Testimonials

Inadequate leadership is one of the most common causes of startup and scaleup failure. *Legendary Leadership in Scaleups* is the go-to leadership guide for founders looking to level up their leadership capabilities and is critical for those that support them. Mary's real-world insights into what makes founders successful make for compelling reading.

Jamie Pride, author,

Unicorn Tears: Why Startups Fail & How To Avoid It

As a founder/CEO, hiring the right team is your most crucial responsibility. The most important thing is to hire a team that not only fits, but adds to your culture and complements the rest of the team. *Legendary Leadership in Scaleups* helps you discover and build the right team to execute your strategy.

Michael Batko, CEO,

Startmate

For a founder, investing in your own leadership isn't a choice, it's a necessity. Your startup can only scale at the speed of your own development. Get ahead of the curve, read this book and forge your own path.

Paul Naphtali, co-founder and managing partner,

Rampersand VC

Leadership capability is the cornerstone in building revenue in complex technical environments. *Legendary Leadership in Scaleups* guides founders to develop the capability to strategically lead their team and lift performance across the business. This book provides the roadmap for you to tackle the difficult decisions head-on and quickly address your leadership capability challenges. It is the book you need to reset your role and reputation as the founder, as you and your business transition to the next level.

Jennifer Kenny, Human Innovation speaker,
CEO of 100 Capacity, founding LP of How Women Invest

Peppered with insights from numerous well-known scaleup leaders, Mary has captured the essence of what separates the legendary leaders from the liabilities. If you're a scaleup founder or senior leader you need this book! It contains well-researched practical advice that's battle-tested with successful scaleup leaders, ensuring you're armed with the tools and roadmap to be a legendary scaleup leader.

Shane Williams, technology leadership expert,
in scaleups

Legendary Leadership in Scaleups is indispensable reading for every founder moving from their successful startup to navigating the scaleup phase. The wonderfully written insights and tips in this book will help you develop greater self-awareness of your impact, understand the roles you need around you, and how your own role needs to change. There are enormous challenges when transitioning and succeeding at the scaleup stage. To every founder out there, keep this book close at hand. It's a must-read for anyone motivated to improve their legacy as a successful entrepreneur.

Richard Wyles, founder and CEO,
Totara Learning

Legendary Leadership in Scaleups

Legendary Leadership in Scaleups

Mary Butler

Published by Mary Butler

First published in 2022 in Melbourne, Australia

Copyright © Mary Butler

www.marybutler.net
Melbourne, Victoria

The moral rights of the author have been asserted.

Edited by Jenny Magee

Illustrations by Sam Bell, Administar

Typeset by BookPOD

ISBN: 978-0-6455627-0-5 (paperback)
ISBN: 978-0-6455627-1-2 (ebook)

NATIONAL LIBRARY OF AUSTRALIA

A catalogue record for this book is available from the National Library of Australia

To Bill, who makes all this possible.

Contents

HOW YOU LEAD PEOPLE HAS THE GREATEST IMPACT

Introduction

First things first

You had a great idea that you wanted to take to the world. Your mates wanted in, so you hired them. It was fun and exciting. No one cared about the long days and nights or the excessive consumption of pizza. It was only you and your tight crew. You were on a mission and would do anything to make it succeed.

Then you started to grow, and you noticed some cracks. You had a vision, but it wasn't turning out quite as you hoped. People had plenty of opinions, which was fine, but they were creating tension among the team. They looked to you for direction, but you just wanted to code.

Now the team is frustrated with your (lack of) leadership. And you are getting frustrated with them. The people you need, want out.

Everyone is starting to cross over each other's work. Direction is poor and expectations are missing. There are no boundaries.

You keep trying to patch up the cracks. But you don't want to ask for help or advice. You don't trust anyone enough for that.

Some people's output standards are dropping. Others have reached the limit of their capabilities, but you don't want to let them go.

It's all having a negative impact on your business. You're feeling overworked, overwhelmed, and overstretched. You're the leader of this business. People are looking to you to make things right. You need to make some tough calls. But what to do?

I'm here to help. Hang in there. You've got this.

Don't let your leadership be a problem

You start your business with the best of intentions. Amazing ideas. Grand plans. Big ambitions.

And then you need people to help you realise those dreams.

At some point, people become the problem, not the solution. But, as the saying goes, it's not them; it's you.

I hear plenty of concerns from the startups I work with.

Founders say:

> I feel stuck in a state of overwhelm, but I don't want to let go.
>
> I'd rather be doing product development than dealing with the people stuff.
>
> I want to define and design my role to support 'where to from here'.
>
> This business is growing rapidly, I need to pause and recalibrate.
>
> There's tension with my co-founder(s) over alignment.
>
> Our culture and brand are drifting and losing focus.

Senior leaders and exec teams say:

" ───────────────────────────────

There's a lack of people leadership capability.

We feel stuck. We can't make decisions to move forward.

We aren't clear about our roles.

There's high risk and high impact if we lose key technical capability.

It's hard to find the right people in today's job market.

Business is operating at breakneck speed, and we're band-aiding the challenges.

─────────────────────────────── "

VCs and investors say:

" ───────────────────────────────

We want to support founders in our portfolio, but they're not hearing us.

The company is burning our money. We want to help them.

The founders and leadership team are not aligned.

Founders need to let go of old ideas to drive performance.

Key relationships need attention, reputations are being challenged.

Founders must make tough calls about holding on to their mates or the 'brilliant jerks'.

─────────────────────────────── "

Like it or not, founders are people leaders

So, you've founded a successful business, one of the ten per cent who got it right. You discovered, created, or designed something outstanding that the world needs and wants. Things will never be the same again. That is amazing. Congratulations!

You're definitely a legend in your field and your area of expertise. Unfortunately, this doesn't mean you're a successful leader of people – you might even be a liability. It's one area where you might need some help.

Regardless of your legendary status as the founder, CEO, CTO, head of product, or CMO, how you lead people has the greatest impact on the whole business. And now more than ever, with a skills shortage and the rapidly increasing cost of hiring, you want to create an environment that attracts the right people and builds engagement to help your business succeed.

Founder liability statistics, compiled by CB Insights in June 2021, show six of the top twenty reasons for startup failure are directly related to the founder's role as leader of people.[1]

What are they?

1. Founder lacks passion
2. Founder lacks focus
3. Founder burnout
4. Founder didn't use the network
5. Disharmony among team and investors
6. Didn't have the right team.

In his book *Unicorn Tears,* Jamie Pride wrote, 'founder failure contributes more than any other factor to startup failure'.[2]

Warning! Becoming a liability may happen gradually. You might not be aware of it, but to your team, it may feel like death by a thousand cuts.

To prevent this from happening to your business, you must invest in developing yourself as a leader to scale your capability and capacity as you scale your business.

Startup books forget people strategy

Where do you learn the people side of your business? Most new leaders start by reading books on the topic before realising that they really need a leadership coach.

Many books on startups and scaling fail to value the importance of people leadership. The role of developing founder self-awareness, growing the right team and building the right infrastructure to drive business growth is under-recognised.

You'll know this is true if you look at your bookshelves.

> *The Fail-Safe Startup*. Tom Eisenmann provides practical tips on growing your business with funding, partners, technology, and customers but has a limited focus on the growth of self or growth of the right team.[3]

> *Disciplined Entrepreneurship*. Bill Aulet writes about twenty-four steps to a successful startup, but people don't rate a mention until around page 261.[4]

> *The Start-up J Curve* by Howard Love includes only three pages on people strategy, broadly discussing hiring ahead of the curve.[5]

The Startup Checklist. Only one of David S. Rose's twenty-five steps relates to people leadership.[6]

The Lean Startup by Eric Ries pays little attention to the need for a people strategy.[7]

These are great books, but they lack an essential ingredient of startup leader success.

Liability or legend? It's your choice

I wrote this book to ensure you don't become a liability in your own business.

Leading people is hard work. It's not why you started the business. It's frustrating and messy, and you'd rather be doing anything else.

Without learning how to be a strategic people leader, you risk everything you've worked so hard to achieve.

It's time for a practical approach to getting the best out of your people so you can become a legendary leader. One who leads people strategically.

A leader who attracts (and keeps) the right people.

A leader who is respected by their peers.

A leader whose ideas and acumen are balanced with their awesomeness.

That's what I want for you. It's what your people – your teams, execs, co-founders, VCs and investors – want for you too.

After all, it flows onto them when you are a legend.

Like it or not, you are always working with people, building relationships with your co-founders, team, customers, investors, the board, and the community.

It's your choice to be a liability or a legend with those people.

If you want your business to scale, strategically leading and communicating will be the key to your success.

Sheryl Sandberg, the former COO of Facebook, wrote: 'Leadership is about making others better as a result of your presence and making sure that impact lasts in your absence.'[8]

Founders can become overwhelmed and overstretched with the variety of work it takes to scale. While you just want to code, meet potential customers, or build marketing strategies, you find yourself doing lots of everything else, and (let's be honest) probably not very well.

You can't continue to be everything to everyone. The thing that's taking most of your time is likely the people stuff. You find yourself dealing with the day-to-day issues of who wants to work from home, who's not getting on with the others and who's not doing the work they were brought in to do. It's relentless, right?

Under this pressure, you can start to become a bottleneck. You don't want to lose control. You get deep into the weeds. You second-guess your decisions. You won't let anyone help you, and you won't make the tough calls. You are becoming a liability.

You choose. Do you want to make the shift from liability to legend?

Liability	Legend
Lacks self-awareness	Seeks feedback to reduce blind spots
Becomes a controlling bottleneck	Learns to let go, engages the team
Refuses support	Seeks help to lift capability
Makes too many assumptions	Provides clear expectations
Buries deep in the weeds	Leads strategically
Is suspicious, and afraid of the tough call	Creates a culture of trust and connection

Model 1: Liability or legend?

Be the strategic leader

While you should clearly not be dealing with the day-to-day people stuff, you can't avoid managing people and building key relationships. No matter what title you operate under (CEO, CMO, CPO), you must learn to lead people strategically. That is, make timely decisions, address challenges as they arise, and set the direction for your business.

> *'One thing I've learned in my 15 years of being*
> *a CEO is that strategy is 90 percent execution*
> *— and 90 percent of execution is people.'*
> – Gary Burnison, CEO, Korn Ferry[9]

Stepping out from the daily operations and becoming a strategic leader will make you a legendary leader.

Your Legendary Leader Roadmap

I've designed this book as a roadmap. You already have a product roadmap, but your business will likely fall victim to you without a clear leadership roadmap.

The easiest path is to make all the common founder mistakes (more on that later); it takes hard work and deep reflection to recognise when you might become a liability to your business.

By investing time, energy, and effort in developing yourself as a leader in your business, this book will set you on the path to becoming a legendary leader.

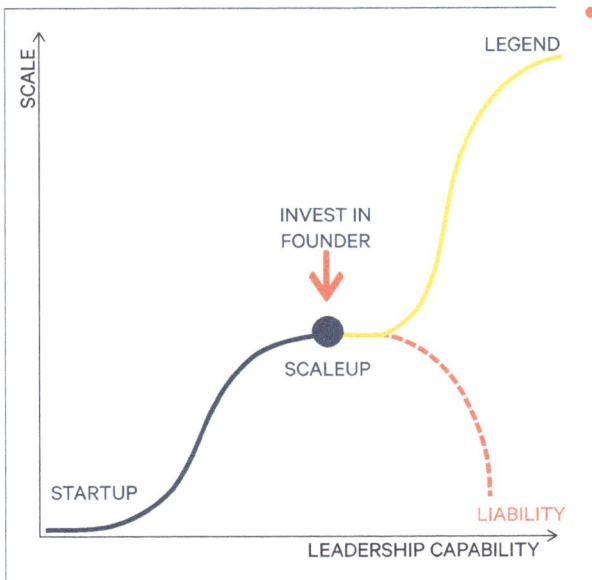

Model 2: Will you be a liability or a legend?

There are five parts to the **Legendary Leader Roadmap:**

Part One: Roadblocks: What's getting in your way?

Part Two: Reputation: Who do you want to be?

Part Three: Role: What do you really want to be doing?

Part Four: Relationships: How do you relate and connect with the people in your community?

Part Five: Right Team: How do you build a team with the right people to help you scale?

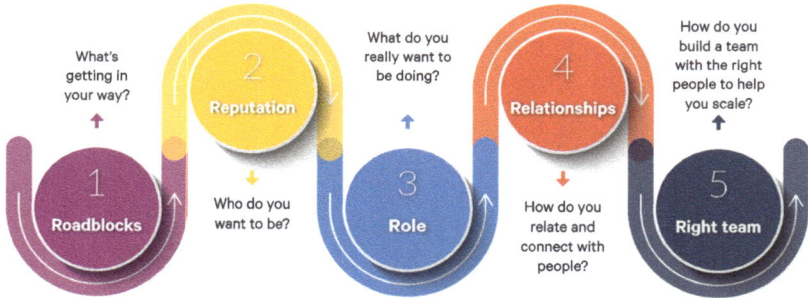

Model 3: Legendary Leader Roadmap

A true legend

The founder/CEO of a successful global tech scaleup was eager to remain across all the decisions in the business, right down to the transactional. He tended to dig deep into the weeds, 'drop a bomb' and leave. While his intentions were good, the impact on the team meant regular distraction, frustration, and confusion.

He needed to re-establish his role and reputation as CEO, responsible for the strategic leadership of the business. A big part of his learning was trusting his team and learning to let go.

A particular strategic decision required him to address some team structure challenges. Rather than holding on to (unhappy) people who no longer served the strategy or culture of the business, he made the tough call to let go of four employees.

These roles did not need to be re-filled, and the departures resulted in savings of more than AU$300,000.

The shift in the team's engagement was palpable, and the CEO's reputation as a strategic leader grew exponentially.

Getting on the path

There is so much to share about becoming a legendary leader. Each person will have different strengths to leverage, different areas for development, and different teams, cultures and support. There is no 'one-size-fits-all' solution.

If you've picked up this book, you're probably already overwhelmed with information and advice, so I want to make this book easy to use.

I discussed this roadmap approach with Colin McLeod, professor and executive director of the Melbourne Entrepreneurial Centre at The University of Melbourne. He commented that founders must have a passion for the journey of entrepreneurship, not just the outcome.

To help you move along your legendary leader roadmap, throughout this book, you will be given suggestions to consider or address. It's your Legend List.

Founders often ask me for the three key actions they need to take, so that's what I'm giving you. But you should also create your own Legend List as you work through the book. You decide what your list needs to be.

This book is chock-full of practical steps and tools to support your path to legendary leadership.

While we follow a roadmap, no two people's challenges will be the same. Each leader's roadblocks will be unique. But once you understand what's getting in your way, you can go straight to the section that will provide a solution to your challenge.

Legend List

1 Identify the current leadership capability roadblocks that are getting in your way.

2 Create your Legend List to tackle the hard stuff quickly.

3 Build a plan of action to deliver great results for you and your business.

LEGENDARY LEADERSHIP

→ IS ABOUT ←

STRATEGICALLY

LEADING PEOPLE

Everything has consequences

How you lead people has the greatest impact on the work environment for the whole business.

It is your responsibility to lead the right team to enable you to scale. You cannot avoid it, do it badly, or outsource it.

What happens if you don't step up?

In personal terms, it will damage your reputation and status in the community. You will be vulnerable to investors and the board, and you might even be forced to step down.

The business could lose key and specialised talent who are not easily replaced. You will fail to scale, and you won't be able to secure funding/IPO.

Investors back the jockey, not the horse

Founders often misunderstand and underestimate the importance of their role in leading their business and securing funding. In conversation with Paul Naphtali, co-founder and managing partner of Rampersand VC, he told me that he sometimes sees something in the founder that they don't see in themselves. VCs look to the founder for leadership capability and how they can lead their business into the future.

Having an amazing idea or concept doesn't mean you will have a successful business – or one that investors will be keen to invest in. Leading your business is not all about the operations, panel presentations, product development, and go-to-market strategy. It involves leading your team and building a solid leadership team to help you scale.

Investors want to see that you can lead your business and not be a liability.

By investing in yourself as a people leader, you will:

- Build a strong team and support network
- Fulfil your potential, as well as that of your business
- Be one of only twenty-five per cent of venture-backed companies that return cash to their investors[10]
- Scale your business with the time and space to do the work you want to do.

A legendary leader attracts talent

With the current global talent scarcity, a legendary leader is essential in attracting talent. If you are not taking responsibility for the strategic leadership of your business, the market will know. Glassdoor quickly lets potential candidates know about liability behaviours within your business.

Managing skills gaps and replacing talent is expensive. You cannot afford to take this lightly. An article in the Australian Financial Review in June 2021 indicated that the cost of hiring skilled software developers, security specialists and data experts has increased by about thirty per cent in Australia in just twelve months.[11]

You cannot continue to scale without focusing on leadership. It's short-sighted to assume that your product or tech is enough to attract the right talent. After all, it's a buyer's market, and the world is full of amazing products and tech. Employees are looking for a far greater range of benefits in a company; careers, equity, flexible hours, health support, hybrid work schedules, aligned values, environmental awareness, and innovative and inspiring leadership.

If you can't provide all this, start working on getting the right team around you who can!

Legend List

1   What assumptions are you making about your role as leader?

2   What are the consequences to you and your business if you don't step up?

3   Find out what your (potential) investors value in a founder. Ask the question.

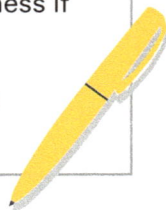

FROM BIG IDEAS

TO

PROCESSES AND GUIDELINES

From startup to scaleup

Let's start with some definitions.

A *startup* is a company in the early stages of business, with big growth plans. It uses innovation to scale rapidly, typically without geographic restrictions. A startup has a perceived demand for its product or service.

A *scaleup* is a high-growth company. The OECD defines high growth as a company that has achieved growth of twenty per cent or more in either employment or turnover, year on year, for at least two years. It also has a minimum employee count of ten at the start of the observation period. A scaleup will typically be through the first round of funding and have reached Series A stage.

The type of people attracted to each business varies across team members and leaders.

Scalable people

A startup is the very early stages of a business, putting an idea or concept into practice to disrupt a market. It's the experimentation stage, where you're still building your tech. There is an opportunity to take more risks as you and your startup are not well known, and there are few customers. As your business grows, consider your funding options.

Startups typically attract people with big ideas who seek challenges and embrace ambiguity and change. Everyone is a generalist, in an all-hands-on-deck kind of way. They tend to resist environments with standards, processes, and established ways of working.

People in scaleups tend to appreciate some adherence to processes and principles. They still enjoy a level of risk and change and pivoting, but their expectations around guidelines for behaviour are higher. The presence of vision statements and values, a more defined culture, an efficient and effective recruitment process, and strong engagement activities are more attractive. These are the scalable people you need in your business as you scale.

What got you here

The biggest challenges for founders moving from startup to scaleup come in understanding roles, hiring the right people, building a strong leadership team, and investing in the infrastructure to support the growth. There is a misconception that founders need to lead everything, be involved in every decision, and have input into every conversation. Unless you adapt your approach, these actions will make you a liability in your business, preventing you from moving to scaleup status. The sooner you recognise this, the better for everyone involved.

In the words of renowned coach Marshall Goldsmith, 'What got you here, won't get you there'. That's particularly true for founders moving into the scaleup phase of their business. If you continue to lead as you've always led, you may well become an impediment. To step up and make the necessary changes for your business to become a scaleup, you'll need to adapt to these legendary leadership lessons.

From startup to scaleup, leading people changes in many ways. Here are five focus areas that demonstrate some simple considerations in your new ways of leading your team:

	From startup	**to scaleup**
Clarity of roles	Who can jump in?	Who's the expert?
Capability	What can they do?	What do they need to be able to do it?
Composition of team	Who do we have?	Who do we need?
Communication	Do we have every-one in the room?	Who actually needs to hear this?
Community	Who do we know?	Who do we need to know?

Model 4: From startup to scaleup

Let's unpack each of the aspects in Model 4.

1. Clarity of roles

Lack of clarity of roles is the most common roadblock to scale. When starting out, you take any help you can get, right? Then as you scale, you realise you need more expertise. You know this, but you are reluctant to hire because you will have to pay for this expertise! As soon as you can afford it (or before), find the expertise you need and stop filling gaps with existing employees who can 'jump in'.

2. Capability

In a small team, you likely know each person's skills. The strengths of each team member have emerged, and everyone does their best. Some people will reach a capability ceiling at some point, and you will need to make a tough call on how to manage this. Fortunately, though, many will be able to grow and expand as your business does. Before it's too late, you will need to establish what capabilities they will need to have to scale as you scale. In Part Five, we will examine how to know what expertise or capability you need – for today and the future.

3. Composition of the team

In addition to technical capability, it is invaluable to understand your team's behaviours, values, teamwork, leadership capabilities, and work ethic. This helps you build the right team for the future. You will need traits, behaviours and qualities that may not be apparent today. Think broadly about how to incorporate the benefits of diversity into your team, including gender, race, age, culture, neurodiversity and people with disabilities.

4. Communication

Communication is about the message, style of delivery, channels and audience. Recognise that not everyone needs to be in the room all the time. Having everyone show up for a discussion is not necessarily the best use of their time. It often means that there are too many opinions, sometimes from people who are not across the context of the discussion. Some people won't be happy to be removed from the discussion, but it's one of those tough calls you'll just have to make.

5. Community

While the startup community is very supportive, it's also quite tight. As it has grown over recent years, I've observed new levels of support and specialised groups forming. At the start, you may not know anyone in the industry or community. As you scale, you'll need to find people you can trust who will guide you in the right direction, including advisors, investors and mentors. Don't wait until it's too late and you're in the middle of a massive crisis with no one to ask for help.

Legend List

1 Establish who can and can't scale as your business scales.

2 Get very clear on role structure and boundaries.

3 Consider the five focus changes of scale and your role as a leader.

FROM

GARAGE

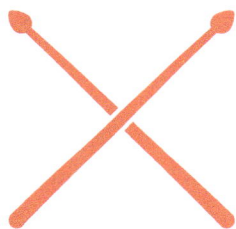

BAND

TO

JAZZ
BAND

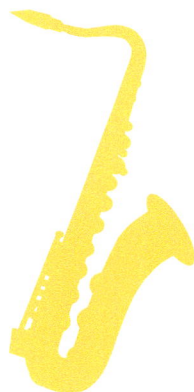

From garage band to jazz band

In his memoir, *The Storyteller*,[12] Dave Grohl shares a story from his early music career during the 1980s. Each Sunday, Dave and his mother attended a jazz workshop at a local venue called One Step Down in Washington DC. Dave tells of his first (and only) structured music lesson from the jazz great Lenny Robinson.

Trying to impress, Dave gave his all in what he called 'cacophonous minutes of disastrous soloing...in its raw, rhythmless glory'. Aware of this, and most embarrassingly, Lenny responded, 'First of all, you're holding your sticks backwards'.

While Dave had natural talent as a drummer, he had been winging it. He learned his craft through listening to tapes of his favourite musicians and replicating what he heard by drumming his pillow. Once he understood some basic techniques, his drumming capability shifted.

Founding a startup feels a bit like setting up a garage band. All your mates are keen to be involved, you need to find the money to buy some instruments and equipment, and you've landed your first gig, but you really have no idea what you're doing.

As your business grows, you become the band manager. You introduce some basic structures, core principles and guidelines, but with the freedom to be flexible and improvise – more like jazz.

The next growth stage is like an orchestra. This is typically in a corporate environment, led by a conductor. Structures have been established, policies and procedures are in place, and everyone knows exactly what their role is and what's expected of them.

Adapting to the rules of jazz

Learning the rules of jazz, and understanding the language of music, takes hard work. Jazz educator Saul Richardson says these levels are not naturally occurring stages. 'Learning how to play jazz involves learning techniques, skills, concepts, applying theory, and procedures.'[13]

At the scaleup stage, you have likely established product-market fit, secured funding, built your tech stack, put replicable systems in place, and the hierarchies are becoming apparent.

You introduce some structure, and establish rules and guiding principles for leading people and team design.

Let's continue the jazz band analogy.

The band needs an official manager, who could be you, your co-founder, or both. You must work out what that means for you and what are your boundaries. (Who will be CEO?)

You take on new band members, people you don't already know and trust. (Grow the team)

There's creative tension among a few of the bandmates. You bring in a new band member to deal with the people stuff. (HR)

Your guitarist's 'three-chord trick' isn't quite cutting it. You become more discerning about new talent and how they assimilate. (Recruitment and onboarding)

A few people emerge to lead the band and make important decisions. (Leadership team and strategy alignment)

You develop the 'what happens on tour, stays on tour' code. (Culture)

You're seeking more advice from band experts, helping you build the right band with the right talents. (Community building)

How are you adapting to the rules of jazz for your startup to scaleup? What are you consciously keeping open to improvisation?

Legend List

1 Are you holding your sticks backwards? Are you still winging it?

2 What principles and guidelines are you beginning to implement as you scale?

3 Are you clear on how moving into the jazz phase will impact your team and how you lead?

THE

CRACKS

OF

SCALE

The cracks of scale

As your business grows, cracks start to form. These can be anything from inefficient processes and cloudy role definitions to personality clashes and leadership challenges. You just want to get on with your day, do your work, secure funding and scale. But these cracks must be addressed before they consume your business.

In an article, *'Give Away Your Legos' and Other Commandments for Scaling Startups*, Molly Graham (ex-early Google and Facebook) discusses the challenges of scaling.[14] 'At 50 people, everything that used to come naturally is now a struggle. And as a new leader, you start getting difficult questions that you've never had to answer before.'

You might be getting asked for career paths, engagement surveys, and performance discussions. These can't be ignored; you must put the infrastructure in place to support this. Well, not you personally, but you must ensure it is done.

Prevent cracks from becoming chasms

How? By becoming a legendary leader, of course. Many challenges arise when moving from startup to scaleup. They don't all appear at once and are not always obvious. Sometimes things happen, and you realise later it's because you're growing and don't have the infrastructure to manage it. Some of the more prominent challenges involve wavering levels of trust and confusion around ownership and responsibilities of tasks and teams. Role clarity is always big on the challenge list, as is inconsistent messaging due to uncertainty and the struggle to manage and lead bigger and more diverse teams.

How do you address this?

Start with you

Put your oxygen mask on before you help others. How can you develop others if you aren't developing yourself first?

As your business has grown, who have you become? Are you being true to yourself and your ideas and beliefs?

Who do you want to be? What is important to you – your values, beliefs, qualities? What is your personal brand? How would you like to be described, internally and externally?

Now is also the time to get clear about who does what. Start with yourself. What's the work you want to do? And not do? What is the right work? What's essential? Define your boundaries and communicate them.

In a 2022 LinkedIn post, author Greg McKeown wrote, 'Essentialism isn't about getting more done in less time. It's about getting only the right things done.'[15]

Change your communication

As a smaller business, you had everyone in the room for every conversation and every decision. As you scale, this is inefficient, ineffective, unsustainable, impractical, and expensive.

Decide who really needs to hear the message and have input. You can't continue to involve everyone in every conversation. It's time to make some tough calls. It won't be easy, but it must be done.

Scale your team

To scale your business, you will also need to scale your team – the right team.

Old ways of working where you hired your mates (i.e. people just like you) won't enable your business to grow. Take the opportunity to hire the right people with the right skills to fill the gaps.

Bring in strengths you didn't realise you needed. Identify the team that will support your future strategy, not just your current operations.

In a private conversation, Dragan Petrovic, co-founder of Nura Headphones, agreed. 'I think scalability is more about enabling a team, providing direction for a team, to do something at a scale that an individual can't.'

Build your community

As you scale, consider who is in your network and who you know in the community.

Who are the investors, board members, customers, key talent, networks, ecosystem supports, technical groups, and panel members? Whose advice and support can help you succeed?

There is no expectation for you to know how to do everything. Anyone who tries to scale without a support network will fail.

To prevent the cracks from becoming a chasm, prioritise the changes that need to happen and action them.

Legend List

1   What cracks are you ignoring?

2   Prioritise the changes that need to happen.

3   Action those changes to prevent a chasm.

Part One

Roadblocks

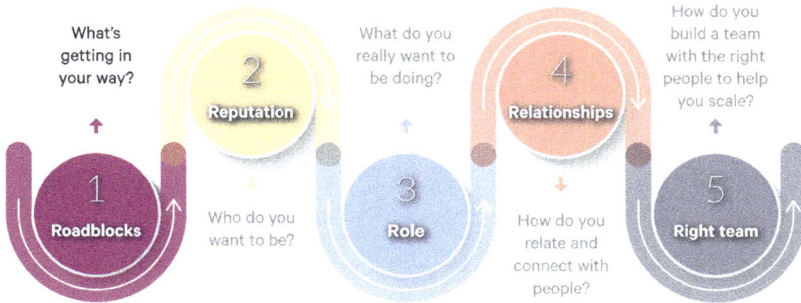

Something's not working

It often feels there is so much going on with distractions, deadlines, and launch dates that it's hard to step back and assess what's working and what's not.

But being a people leader is your job. As a scaleup legend, you lead your people, set direction, and support them to achieve the business goals that represent success for you.

How you've been leading until now has worked. It's been all-hands-on-deck, and people have managed to work this way. But as you scale, more challenges become apparent, and your team can't keep going.

I'm more often contacted for help by the leadership team or the head of People and Culture (P&C) than the founder. That's because the team experiences the greatest challenges, and they need you to be able to step up as a legendary leader.

Are you the roadblock?

Frankie, the P&C lead in a high-growth tech company, called me in a panic because they felt things were getting out of control. The co-founders were relentlessly driving the leadership team to deliver in a fast-paced environment with no relief. As they were not prepared to assess their leadership style and capabilities, they were becoming liabilities to their business.

With rapid recent growth, the business was continually operating at breakneck speed.

The flat structure meant some managers had a large number of direct reports. These reports were hired quickly, and the managers didn't have the skills to manage them effectively. They were quickly losing highly skilled team members, which exposed the business to risk.

Frankie invited me to meet with the leaders across the business, including the co-founders who initially resisted. Apparently, they didn't need help.

We discussed areas that needed to be addressed from business and people leadership perspectives. We agreed that scaling was not sustainable for the business at this pace. There was no clear direction or focus. Instead, there was a culture of reacting rather than taking time to provide considered and informed responses. Short-cuts and band-aiding had become the normal way of operating. There was an urgent need for role clarity and defining expectations.

From a people leadership viewpoint, the struggles were becoming too hard for many managers. There was a clear need to ensure alignment across the leadership team, which required a high level of communication capability.

Some people managers had been hired without management capability or experience. They couldn't continue to move the business forward without providing people managers with the tools and support to lead their teams. Some people felt stuck and could not navigate or unblock themselves to take ownership of their roles. It wasn't easy to ask for help.

People described not feeling empowered to do their work autonomously. That meant key decisions were delayed and people felt undervalued. They had hired to fill gaps, mainly in technical abilities, without considering behavioural capabilities.

There was a request to pay special attention to wellbeing in the business. The co-founders believed everything was under control, and people had the option of a positive work-life balance. While the co-founders worked excessive hours, they didn't recognise that this created a similar expectation on the team. This was even though they shared that this was not their expectation.

It took a lot of convincing from the leadership team to get the co-founders engaged in the program of work. There was plenty of scepticism at first, but they couldn't continue to ignore the pleas from the team. We worked together to help the co-founders to recognise that their leadership style was a roadblock to their business. Fortunately, they eventually took the opportunity to learn how to move from liability to legend.

Your misconceptions

When you started out, there was only you and maybe your co-founder. Then, you recruited a few mates. Now your business is growing rapidly, yet you want to keep working the same way and keep the same vibe. But you know deep down, you can't....

There are a bunch of roadblocks in your way, and they are making you into a liability.

Which of these misconceptions are you operating under?

? If I keep slogging it out, things will get better. I've done it before, I'm just a little stuck. (This is known as the 'halo effect'.)

? Everyone respects my style of leadership. It worked for Jobs, Musk and Bezos; it'll work for me. No need to adapt or grow.

? I'm fully self-aware. I've no blind spots. Nothing to learn here, folks!

? Of course, people love working here! There is no risk of them leaving. We have ping pong, bean bags and Friday drinks! What's not to love?

? I must be all things to everyone; the founder, CTO, advisor, head of product, head of marketing, head of people, the inspirational CEO.

? I'm expected to manage all of the day-to-day people stuff. I'm a bit exhausted playing whack-a-mole, but it comes with the founder territory, doesn't it?

? We all know what role we're in and who's doing what. There's no need for hierarchy or reporting lines, even though we're growing rapidly. Everyone likes the informality of it.

? Everyone likes my mates! Sure, maybe they're not the best fit anymore, and they're getting a bit disgruntled. But they were here at the start, so I can't ask them to move on. It wouldn't be right.

? Everyone's aligned and fully engaged. We're all in sync. No need to check in and confirm.

? We can communicate just like we always have, even though we've grown to more than thirty people. We're family here, and if someone misses something, somebody else will pick it up.

? I can outsource the big decisions. No one likes having challenging conversations and making tough calls. Someone else can manage that.

? There's no need to involve anyone else in this discussion. Investors and advisors could probably help, but why bring them into this conversation?

If some of those resonated with you, you may be a liability as a leader. It's not your fault, but it is your choice to do something about it. Will you be a liability or a legend with your people?

In the following four sections, we'll explore the roadblocks in your business, focusing on your reputation, role, relationships, and the right team. Removing these roadblocks will help you become a legendary leader.

Legend List

1 What misconceptions are you operating under?

2 Ask your leadership team if you are a roadblock. It might be a blind spot for you.

3 Have you chosen to be a legendary leader? What does that look like for you?

Reputation roadblocks

'The amateur has a long list of fears. Near the top are two: solitude and silence. The amateur fears solitude and silence because she needs to avoid, at all costs, the voice inside her head that would point her toward her calling and her destiny. So she seeks distraction. The amateur prizes shallowness and shuns depth.'

– Steven Pressfield, Turning Pro[1]

What do people really say about you?

Mike's business was growing fast. Everything was changing, and he was trying to keep up. But his vision didn't match what was going on. He started his business to do work he loved, but it was starting to feel like he was losing his way. And maybe (subconsciously) he was behaving in ways that were not always helpful. He wanted to be involved in all the decisions but was rarely available for discussions. He knew that issues were arising, and he was avoiding them. He was exhausted from trying to do everything.

He was busy. He was too busy to talk. He was falling into work where he felt comfortable and useful. Yet he knew he wasn't doing the important work. He was a bit stuck and needed a reset and some direction.

Mike was becoming a liability.

Take a moment...

Is Mike you? Is this your reputation? How would you describe your leadership style? How would your peers describe you? And your team? And the broader community? What are people really saying about you? What is your reputation?

You might feel stretched and overwhelmed and try to hide this from people. But it always seeps through. If not the obvious, visible way, it will present as you getting frustrated, creating arguments, or spending long days at the office. It all feeds into your reputation and how people see you.

Are you experiencing:

- fear of disappointing yourself, your family and your team?
- expectations to behave in a way that doesn't align with your thinking?
- constant stress and exhaustion?
- overstretched, overwhelmed, and overworked?
- feeling out of your depth?
- feeling undervalued because you're not doing work that's important to you?

WHAT ARE PEOPLE REALLY SAYING ABOUT YOU?

Are you difficult to work with because you're:

- ? protective of 'your baby' because it's being called ugly?

- ? dependent on your genius to get you through?

- ? becoming controlling and even a bottleneck for decisions?

- ? focused on the short term, stuck in the operational work, and not leading strategically?

- ? losing patience and negatively impacting the team?

- ? letting your ego get in the way, and you can't let go?

Do you need to hold up the mirror? Are you:

- ? tied to old beliefs and old ideas?

- ? experiencing emerging blind spots that are being ignored (or unrecognised)?

- ? in denial that there's a problem, and you're avoiding the issues?

- ? feeling like you don't fit in here anymore?

- ? ignoring advice and not trusting your team?

- ? lacking the humility to realise what's truly going on?

As Verne Harnish writes in *Scaling Up,* 'The bottleneck is always at the top of the bottle.'[2]

If any of this is true for you, start considering what is important to you? What is it that you truly value? Why are you here, doing all this? It's time to reset and get back to basics.

Developing your leadership capability will improve your image and reputation and help prevent you from becoming a liability.

Legend List

1   What do people really think of you? Ask them.

2   Is that what you want to be known for? If not, what are you going to do about it?

3   It's time to hold up the mirror.

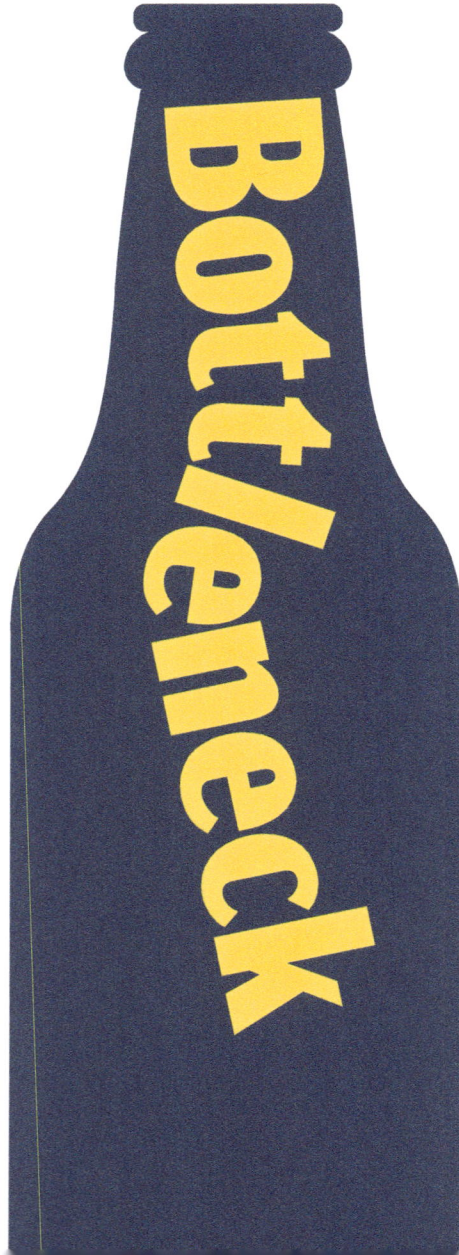

DON'T BE A

Bottleneck

Role roadblocks

Growth demands a new level of work

You started with an idea that has taken off. That is fabulous. You can't believe how successful you are! You're great at product development, marketing, design, software development, or engaging clients, but you find you're not doing quite as much of that work these days. As a result, you're not feeling very fulfilled.

Growth demands a new level of work you're not necessarily familiar with. It requires you to step up, lead, and be strategic. Be honest. Would you hire yourself for that position?

Get out of there

Do you find yourself diving into work you're comfortable with rather than addressing the strategic challenges of your business?

When you try to get into the details of the product or marketing or tech, do you find you're annoying your team? They want you out of there. You know you can add value, but they don't want to listen. (Hint: it might be a case of too many chiefs!) Or you're coming in with half the information at the last minute and trying to change things when informed, collaborative decisions have already been made.

The impact of this on you and your team can be devastating. You might be miserable, but you're making your team miserable too. You are doing lots of everything and doing nothing well. No one (including you) really knows what you're supposed to be doing or not doing.

You may have found yourself getting dragged into all the people issues. There are so. Many. People issues! It's relentless. Why do you care who gets the seat by the window? Or why Sam isn't talking to Phil? Or which person gets to have the day off? All that he said/she said/they said stuff.

Is all the decision-making still coming through you, no matter how (un)important? Are you holding things up because you just can't get to everything? But you're not quite ready to trust someone else to make the decisions? Or you are ready, but there's no one ready to hand over to.

It's possible you're being transitioned into the role of CEO, which requires exemplary people leadership skills and a strategic mind. Are you the right person for that job? Would you hire yourself for that position?

In conversation, Dragan Petrovic, co-founder of Nura Headphones, said, 'Particularly as a domain expert, (the founder) needs to do things differently from what they were doing before. They need to move to a higher level of abstraction and not get into the same level of detail because that doesn't scale.'

If you continue trying to be everything to everyone, doing everything, being a bottleneck, and not letting go, you will become a liability. A role roadblock.

Legend List

1   Would you hire yourself into your position?

2   Do you know your strengths and what happens when you're not using them?

3   What work do you need to let go of?

RELATIONSHIPS

Relationship roadblocks

How you lead and relate to people has a huge impact on the success of your business. Consider your relationships with your co-founder, leadership team, broader team, customers, investors, the board, advisors, the market, and the community.

Building a business means having lots of new people in your world. Some you'll enjoy working with, others not so much. Regardless of how you feel about working with people, you must understand and appreciate how to strategically communicate with and lead people and foster those relationships.

I love the quote attributed to actor, comedian, and producer Henry Winkler, that assumptions are the termites of relationships.

Damaging relationships

In an article in Forbes magazine, founder and CEO Arzu Tekir wrote the following. 'Things like poor internal communication, gossiping, micromanagement, small-picture attitudes, and unfriendly competition in the office are hallmarks of a workplace culture that can kill a startup before it has a chance to succeed.'[3]

What are the signs that relationships are being damaged? They fall into the following four categories.

1. Culture

Finger-pointing and blame are normal. Expectations are unclear. There's a culture of making assumptions without conversation. Engagement scores are low and attrition rates are climbing. Culture is drifting and becoming toxic. Leaders don't celebrate success. There is a sense of intolerance and not encouraging questions.

2. Communication

People fire off emails rather than picking up the phone to resolve an issue. There's a lack of clarity of responsibilities and expectations. People are not enabled to do their jobs. Leaders are not communicating or being transparent about what needs to be shared. Important information is lost or blocked. People feel rattled by quick decisions that impact them. Leaders don't include the team in decisions that affect them (where appropriate).

3. Connection

People are losing faith, trust, and loyalty. There's a lack of honesty and transparency. Information is shared via instructions rather than some attempt at collaboration. Leaders are not having difficult conversations or providing effective feedback. There is an assumption about what people know and how they'll react. Expectations are not being managed.

4. Community

The right people aren't in the room. Decision-making bypasses the experts, and information isn't shared with the right people. Leaders don't know where to turn to get support. Their reputation and that of the business are weak in the community.

If these signs of damaged relationships are apparent in your business, they are indications that the leader is becoming a liability. Could this be you? How would you know?

Legend List

1 What are the signs (and causes) of relationship tensions in your business?

2 What are your most important relationships?

3 What are you doing to nurture and develop them?

BEWARE

TEAMS

THAT

GROW

TOO

ORGANICALLY

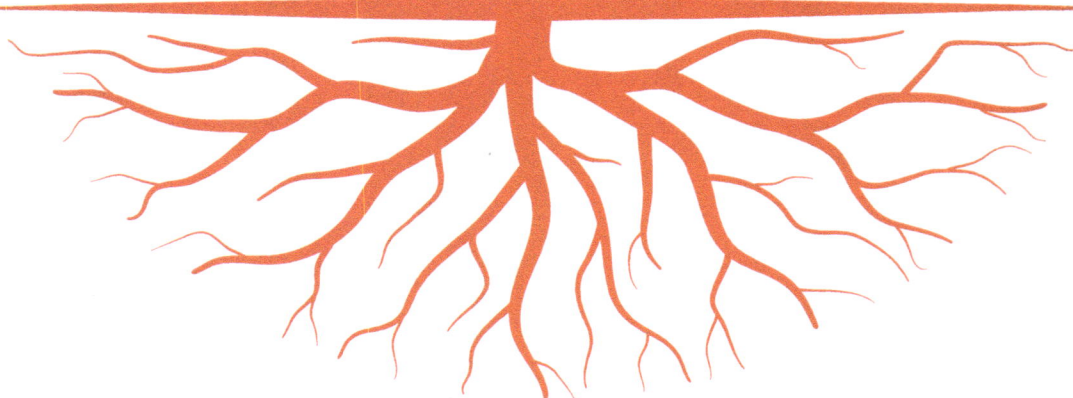

Right team roadblocks

Common mistakes in scaling your team

It's never too early to start considering how your team will look as you scale. You can prevent many pain points, challenges and costs associated with having the wrong team. All it takes is time to establish what capabilities you'll need (technical and behavioural), what culture you want for your business, and how you'll continue to attract the right people.

Perhaps you think you don't know what you need today, so how can you know what you'll need in the future? That's okay, it will continue to evolve, and you can adapt as necessary. Roadblocks occur when you let teams grow too organically.

I discussed the characteristics of a founder and growing the right team with Jane Newton (Martino), consultant, advisor, investor, director, and co-founder of Smiling Mind. She said, 'Too often, ego drives the founder. It takes life experience and humility to step back and reset when things go wrong, to prioritise the things that are important and focus on team and culture.'

These are where things can often go wrong.

1.　Building the wrong team structure

Your team structure has emerged organically. People have absorbed roles they're not qualified for. And now people have crazy titles, doing work they are neither capable of doing nor have the capacity to do.

You hired lots of people just like you – because they get it! But eventually, some don't. They don't have the capability or potential to grow with your business. And you have avoided having tough conversations while ignoring the impact this has on the rest of the team.

The structure isn't aligned to anything (not even the business strategy). You have been filling role gaps and replacing like with like.

There are no frameworks for reference to enable useful performance conversations, like capability and technical frameworks. (This also leads to a lack of role clarity.)

You don't have regular performance or career conversations, maybe you don't see them as important, or they're too corporate-y. The result is that people won't really know how well they're doing and will be surprised to hear they're not making the mark.

In truth, you probably don't want structures, reporting lines, and all that corporate stuff. You believe everyone wants to keep the 'family vibe'. But as you grow, you realise they're not family. It's your business.

2. The smartest people are not always the right people

Hiring the best and the brightest people at the highest salary levels is a bad idea. They absorb all the available salary, then get bored and frustrated doing lower-level work, and are impossible to manage. Instead of always hiring the smartest people, try growing and developing them from inside the business.

3. Making costly hiring mistakes

Your hiring plan (if there is one) is not aligned with any business objective.

You have a short-term focus.

You need people quickly, so you hire fast and fire slow. Or you have not fired at all and are still carrying the wrong people.

You have no criteria for hiring and don't take an holistic approach. For example, hiring for technical skills and not accounting for behavioural skills or experience because that's too expensive.

There is a temptation to rehire the mistakes, replacing old with new versions of the wrong people.

As author Ben Horowitz explains, when you needed an expert, 'you hired for lack of weakness rather than for strengths'.[4] This is even more common when hiring is by consensus.

4. Not guiding the culture

You have no company values, guiding principles, ways of working, or whatever you want to call them. These are the anchor for all behaviours. Without them, you have no point of reference to call out bad behaviour or celebrate good behaviour! Because defining company values is an inclusive process, it is often a casualty of over-thinking and inflexibility.

Culture evolves organically. But what guides that culture? Is it poor behaviour, lack of communication, or bullying? Is this the culture you want? Without direction from you, the culture will take its own path.

5. No clear and attractive Employee Value Proposition (EVP)

There is a global talent shortage, with strong competition for talent. Yet you're not clever in your talent search. You don't have a strong and current EVP. What can you offer potential candidates? What values do you want in the people you hire?

Every company is your competition, so it's essential to be attractive. I know you're doing cool things – so is everyone. Do you know what makes you stand out? Hint: potential candidates will expect attractive benefits, clearly defined career paths, fulfilment of a sense of purpose, and a progressive, supportive work environment.

You don't have an efficient and effective recruitment process. The wrong people are doing the interviewing, and it's taking forever to make a decision. Top candidates won't sit around waiting for you to decide.

6. Ineffective hiring and engagement strategies

In September 2021, I surveyed twenty scaleups in Australia to understand their challenges in attracting and retaining talent. They were experiencing an accelerated shift in the digital landscape, meaning specialised skills were particularly hard to find. And with over-inflated salaries in a competitive market, underqualified staff were overpaid.

The impact of longer time to hire meant being under-resourced for longer. This meant a greater need for rework and led to poor engagement and retention of existing team members.

The main reasons for this happening were a natural reaction to the pandemic and uncertainty about the future. There was no talent pool, loyalty was low, mobility and relocation were barriers, and they just couldn't afford quality hires.

They were all making enormous efforts to overcome these challenges. They noted that some activities were not working well, including fatigue from Zoom catchups, the LinkedIn and SEEK generic approaches, rewriting job ads to suit the availability, and then hiring the wrong people. Convincing people to stay after they decide to leave is almost always a bad idea. They also indicated that referral rewards were not very successful.

Although the survey was done in 2021, little has changed since. The talent scarcity is becoming even more apparent. Figures released by the Australian Bureau of Statistics (June 2022) showed the proportion of vacant jobs at a record high, with around 420,000 vacancies (2.8 per cent). That is nearly double what it was before the start of the pandemic.[5]

It is up to you to address the challenges for your business. Don't think it is an external problem. Many companies are leading the way in developing benefits and ways to attract and retain employees. Why wouldn't candidates come to work with you? Is it because you don't know how to attract them?

Legend List

1. Do you have the right people for your business?

2. What's keeping your existing employees? Or are they at risk of leaving? Ask them.

3. Develop and advertise a compelling Employee Value Proposition.

Part Two

Reputation

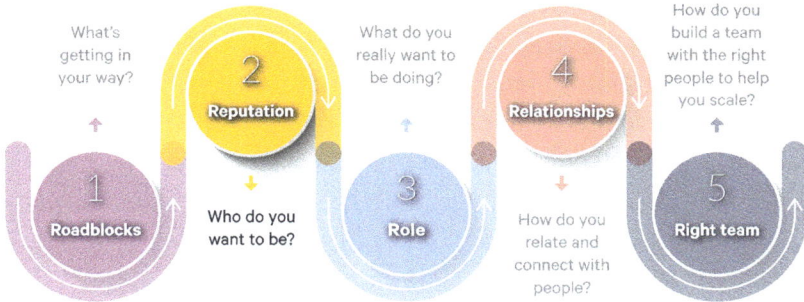

What's getting in your way?

1 Roadblocks

Who do you want to be?

2 Reputation

What do you really want to be doing?

3 Role

How do you relate and connect with people?

4 Relationships

How do you build a team with the right people to help you scale?

5 Right team

I asked Zac Duff, co-founder and CEO of JigSpace, what he would like to be known for. Without hesitation, he replied, 'Being fun to work with and making dope shit'.

I love this – for so many reasons. Zac knows exactly why he does what he does. He is clear and focused, and as a result, he is having massive success with JigSpace. (In 2022, Alfa Romeo F1 Team ORLEN named JigSpace as their official metaverse partner.) So it's no surprise that Zac is one of my all-time favourite founders to work with. (I can have favourites, right?)

A reputation economy

The Cambridge Dictionary Online defines reputation as 'the opinion that people in general have about someone or something, or how much respect or admiration someone or something receives, based on past behaviour or character'.

Our reputation or brand image is other people's perception of us or how they view us. We can't control this, but we can influence it.

It can be challenging. We live in a time of a reputation economy where we are assigned reputation scores, whether we like it or not. Others have expectations of us that we haven't created or necessarily want to conform or adapt to. It's like Uber ratings. Traditionally customers would rate a service provider. Now, the service provider rates us too. We are being assessed all the time.

REPUTATION
IS
PERCEPTION

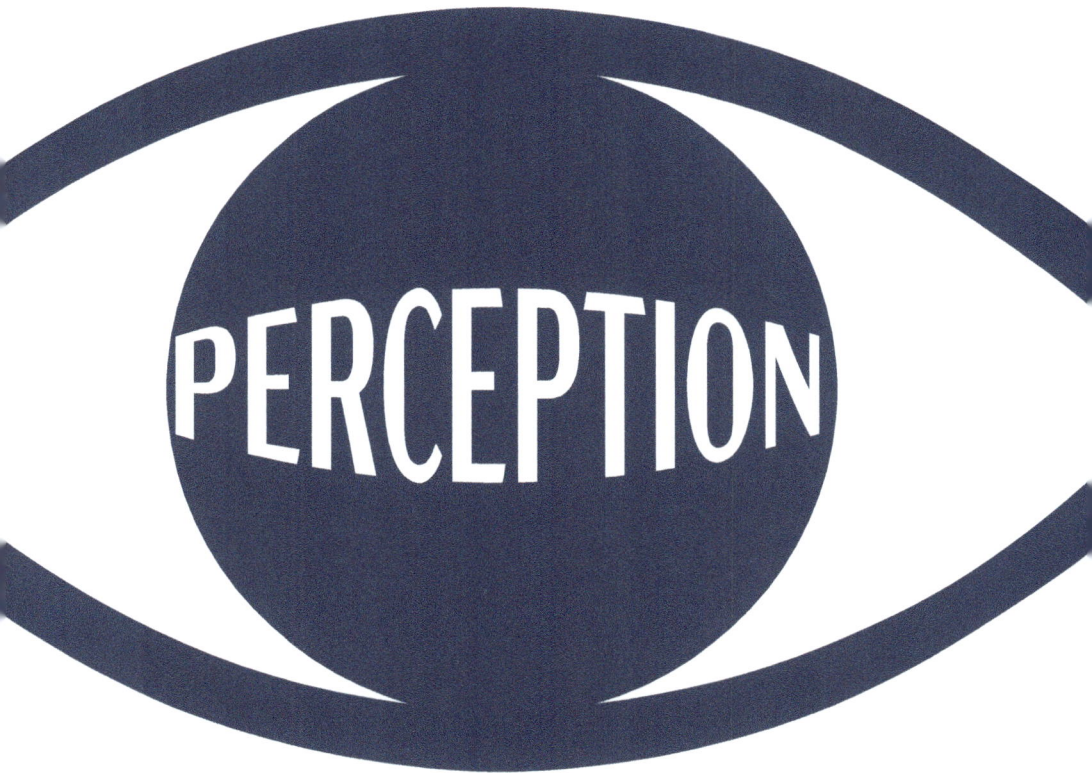

Reputation is perception

Your reputation or image is how you are seen or perceived. We know that perception is reality, so investing in your reputation is incredibly important.

Your reputation comes from your character, identity, credibility, behaviour, appearance, and position in your business and the community. To the outside world, reputation represents you and your company brand.

You're not always going to like what people say about you, but to succeed, as Kate Morris, co-founder at Adore Beauty, told me, 'Founders need to become more resilient; you've got to be able to hear the feedback and cop the rejection'.

How you portray yourself is critical to your success and the success of your business.

How do you show up?

A founder client of mine once shared that when he travelled, he would book the cheapest economy fare, stay in budget hotels, and pack his lunch (okay, not quite). He did it because he was growing his business and didn't want his team to feel he was splurging on luxuries. But it meant that he often missed flights and scheduled meetings. Arriving sweaty and flustered to meet his customers, he was constantly letting himself and his business down. We discussed how this might impact his brand and reputation.

Rather than see him as suitably frugal, maybe his team felt that (aspirationally) that was good as it gets. It wasn't very inspiring.

It also didn't inspire confidence in his customers.

If an investor saw him in a long queue for taxis, probably scrolling emails (but perceived as wasting time on Twitter!), they might feel his time could be better spent.

With some debate, we agreed to a few tweaks to his travel arrangements. He books suitable plane fares and decent accommodation, reflecting his success and rewarding him for his hard work. It means he is no longer rushing and gets proper rest.

He invested in a few pieces of premium, classic clothing and accessories. Subtle but sharp and still aligned with his style (he has a penchant for watches).

He now books a driver to meet him at the airport. That way, he can walk straight into a waiting car without wasting time. He can work comfortably on the way to his meetings and arrive to meet customers fresh and confident. He gets home more quickly and is present for his family. Big wins all around.

Your reputation requires constant focus as it can slip at any time. The greater the foundation, the stronger it will be in times of challenge.

When no one's looking

The Urban Dictionary defines character as 'What a person is really like. Their values, personality, and level of integrity...when no one's looking.'

Your behaviour when no one is looking reflects your moral qualities, values, and beliefs. It affects how you respond to challenges, celebrate success, and support your team in good times and bad. It feeds through everything you do as a leader.

Over a decade ago, author Seth Godin described a linchpin as 'the one person who can bring it all together and make a difference'. He says the linchpin is 'the essential element.... Without the linchpin, the thing falls apart.'[1]

How can you leverage what you know about who you are and how you behave to become the linchpin in your business?

Confidence v competence

How you view yourself as a leader, your self-belief and conviction, impacts how others see you. Being a founder and leader is very challenging, and it's common to feel out of your depth.

In his book *Think Again*, Adam Grant describes the Dunning-Kruger effect, where there is an imbalance between competence and confidence.[2] We see this imbalance in founders and leaders too. The lack of confidence can come from doing work you're not familiar with or not particularly good at. You doubt yourself and are uncertain of your ability to lead, but you're not ready to let go just yet. But you might be holding up the decision-making process, creating bottlenecks and not trusting those around you. This significantly impacts your reputation and the success of your team and your business.

Or maybe you are over-confident in your ability to lead your business. Are you so self-assured that you don't need to listen to anyone else or hire anyone to fill your capability gaps?

Getting the balance of confidence and competence is essential to becoming a legendary leader.

Look in the mirror

Leverage your strengths

While you can't always control your reputation, you can influence it by getting clear on how you want to behave and show up for your team, your investors and your customers. Understand who you want to be in your environment.

Are you sometimes conflicted because it feels like people don't understand what you're trying to achieve? Or perhaps they don't appreciate how you go about fulfilling your vision.

Do the work that is meaningful for you. The work that fulfils your purpose, the reason you started this business.

Do the work that leverages your strengths and capabilities. The work that will make you feel valued in your business.

Consider your impact

How are people experiencing working with you? Are you aware of the impact you're having on them?

It's understandable that you want to protect your business. After all, you created it, and you want to ensure that everyone acts in ways that support your vision.

As your business scales, it might feel like people aren't listening to you, or they don't get why you are frustrated with how they do things.

Consider how you are when it comes to decisions. How important is the decision? Are you the best person to make that decision? Do you have all of the information? Are you the expert in this area? Are all the right people in the discussion? Beware that you're not becoming too controlling or challenging others' decisions.

Are you getting caught up in the day-to-day operational work? As the leader, it's your responsibility to leave the operational functions to those you've hired to do that work. Your job is to take a strategic lead with a longer-term focus.

Sometimes it's necessary to get out of your own way. Your ego is calling the shots, not logic or reason. It might be because you struggle to trust people or to let go.

If this is a challenge for you, and you're losing patience with yourself and your team, it will negatively impact everyone. Consider the effect of your words and actions.

From working with many founders, I can say that most are results-focused. That's why they grow successful businesses. But you can't be so focused on the numbers and results that you alienate those you need around you.

Listen up

Professor Colin McLeod, executive director of the Melbourne Entrepreneurial Centre at The University of Melbourne, says founders must have 'the humility to not have to be right all the time, the humility to accept and learn from failure, and the humility to listen to the opinions of others'. Professor McLeod wants founders to realise that the best advice comes in the form of conversation; it's a two-way street. While advisors will diligently and authentically offer the best advice they can, they will accept that it is your business and your journey, so the decision on what to do is yours.

It may not always feel like it, but most people have your best interests at heart. People want you to succeed. They're not out to see you fail. The main person blocking success is you.

Maybe it's time to reset your vision for your business, to let go of old beliefs and ways of working. Recognise where you're in denial and avoidance mode.

There is always a team of people around you, inside and outside your business, who are willing to give you feedback, support, and advice. They'll help you in your new direction. Trust them.

Have the humility to listen to what's being said, so you can address some of those behaviour challenges. Developing your leadership capability will improve how you view yourself and your reputation. It will help prevent you from becoming a liability.

Elevate your reputation

It's entirely possible that you haven't been in a people leadership position before, so you don't have a reputation as a leader who is a liability or a legend!

That part of your image or brand hasn't yet been created or established. So, this is your opportunity to lift your image to become the leader you want to be. It won't take from who you are – unless, of course, the current image that's working for you is being a rogue, a vagabond, or a deviant....

Steven Pressfield writes in *Turning Pro*, 'We may bring intention and intensity to our practice (in fact we must), but not ego. Dedication, even ferocity, yes. But never arrogance.'[3]

Seek out people you admire

Avoid becoming a liability by getting in front of your reputation early.

In the previous chapter, we looked at opportunities for developing your reputation. What's important to you, and what's your purpose? Who are you in your business? This is the starting point to influencing your reputation.

Think about the people whose presence you *enjoy*. Who makes you feel good to be around them? How do you behave then? What do you do or think differently when you're with them? Do they remove any fear you have about showing vulnerability? Do they give you the confidence to make good decisions? Maybe they help you explore ideas you hadn't previously considered. Perhaps they made you think differently for a far better outcome.

It might be that your leadership style is one of early collaboration with people like this. Rather than expecting to provide all the answers yourself, invite one (or some) of these people into the conversation.

Now, think of people you *admire*. Maybe a manager from a previous career. Or someone in your current circle. What do you admire about them? Are they calm under pressure? How do they react to bad news? Do they keep people's spirits up when there is a crisis? Perhaps they show care for people, recognising when someone needs extra support and making space for them.

What you recognise and admire in others are often the values and traits you'd like to emulate. These are the traits that have currency for you.

I have given this much consideration over my career and have narrowed it down to two things.

Firstly, I am always conscious of the values that are most important to me, particularly trust. I need to trust my clients and colleagues, and I also need to feel trusted. Trust and be trusted. I cannot work with clients whose behaviours or culture contravene my values.

Secondly, I admire people who have fun and don't take things too seriously. They know when to let go and have a laugh. They're the people I like to work with. That's also what I would like people to see in me and how it would be to work with me.

REPUTATION.

YOU CAN'T

CONTROL

IT,

BUT YOU CAN

INFLUENCE

IT.

Invest in your reputation

Sarah is one of many founders I work with in exploring how to shift reputation. In our recent meeting, she hesitated to dive into the reputation discussion. 'Why does it matter? I am who I am, and my team likes me, so why do I need to change for anyone?'

I reassured her that she could remain true to herself and her values, as that had got her this far. Her image was already positive and strong, but there's always room for improvement. Her business was scaling rapidly, and she needed to scale with it.

Sarah's business is three years old. She is in the midst of fundraising, and things are looking good. Her team of sixty people has gone global.

Who is Sarah?

Most of Sarah's experience has been with smaller tech companies, eventually in senior technical roles. She has a master's degree in engineering and has completed many short programs supporting her technology requirements. She has worked for ten years in her particular area of engineering.

Sarah is full of life. She is dynamic and engaging, and her team loves working with her. She is collaborative and supportive.

What's important to Sarah is having a team that loves coming to work and loves what they do. Her business supports climate action and feeds that purpose for her. She hires people with similar beliefs and values.

The challenge is that although Sarah is a senior engineer, she has never led a team. While naturally comfortable leading people, she hasn't had any training or formal development in this area. She is now learning on the job and making rookie errors with big consequences.

The mirror never lies

Using my Discover process, I encourage leaders to request feedback from their team, the board and the investors – where relevant. To learn more about what behaviours she might have been ignoring and to reduce her blind spots, Sarah did an informal 360. She emailed focused, relevant questions to people she trusts and whose feedback and advice she valued (this part was really important).

Here's what she learned:

Her team loves her spontaneity and that she is fully engaged, but the lack of role clarity across the business is leaving them frustrated. There is confusion about who is responsible for what and who makes the final decision. People don't feel empowered or enabled to do their jobs.

Sarah sometimes forgets to include the right people in the conversation. She also tends to make decisions on the fly without much due diligence. In her excitement, she often jumps into projects without all the information, creating a bit of a stir.

Information coming through isn't clear. Messages from Sarah are often vague and not future-focused. There is no strategy for the business, so making plans is becoming difficult.

Sarah's ad hoc communication style is also creating confusion among the team.

Direction is poor. Expectations are not clear.

Sarah's style is to wing it rather than providing well-informed results. This lack of preparation and ambiguity is starting to rattle the board.

Sarah is overworked and not setting a good example for the team. She is becoming short-tempered.

As the team grows, fewer people feel trusted, and sharing work is not done equally.

Her leadership team members are struggling to keep the boat afloat. They are tired of working at break-neck speed while band-aiding as they go. This is not sustainable. They are asking for help.

How did we help Sarah address these challenges?

✓ Sarah got very clear on what was important to her and what was necessary for her to do, and learned to let go of everything else.

✓ She established a new team structure, taking her out of the detail and allowing her to delegate, and lighten her decision-making responsibilities.

✓ She communicated the new role structure to the whole team, so that everyone had clarity.

✓ She worked on improving her communication style, recognising where she needed help.

✓ She engaged the support of her leadership team, who filled in the communication gaps (the detail).

✓ She created an environment where building trust was central to the culture, empowering her team to step up and make decisions.

✓ She designed her work to reduce her hours and spend more time with her family and friends, thus preventing further burnout.

Legend List

1 What is your mirror telling you? What have you been ignoring?

2 Reduce any blind spots by seeking insights into your reputation from people you trust.

3 What small changes can you make to impact your reputation positively?

Part Three

Role

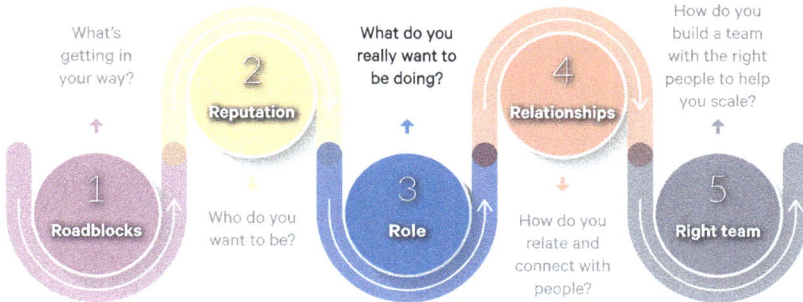

What's getting in your way?

2 Reputation

What do you really want to be doing?

4 Relationships

How do you build a team with the right people to help you scale?

1 Roadblocks

Who do you want to be?

3 Role

How do you relate and connect with people?

5 Right team

Rich or king?

The biggest roadblock to scaling your business invariably comes down to clarity about your role and those of your team. People need to know what you're doing (and not doing). They also want to understand what's expected of them, what they're responsible for, and who to go to with questions and for direction.

In the startup space, there is a lot more room for ambiguity. As you scale, you attract people who like the speed and challenges that come with high growth, but they will want to know their roles and responsibilities. I have seen the tension and clashes that come when people overstep boundaries. And when the boundaries and expectations are unclear, the challenges grow because no one knows how to call them out.

> 'Entrepreneurship is a personal growth
> engine disguised as a business pursuit.'
> – James Clear, author and entrepreneur.[1]

One of the greatest challenges (and opportunities) for a founder is deciding their role in their growing business. An early decision is whether they want to maintain control of their business or want to focus on building financial gains.

In his book, *The Founder's Dilemmas*, Noam Wasserman calls this the wealth versus control dilemma.[2] Elsewhere it is described as the kingdom or the throne, or rich or king.

Founders can, of course, be both. Wasserman calls it the entrepreneurial ideal. Bill Gates (Microsoft), Anita Roddick (Body Shop), and Mark Zuckerberg (Facebook) are good examples, but to be the best at both is unusual. You may have a co-founder where

LACK OF
ROLE CLARITY
IS THE
NUMBER
ROADBLOCK 1

one of you controls running the business while the other focuses on reaching wealth potential and pursuing business opportunities.

If you've built your business by doing everything and making all the decisions, this isn't sustainable as you continue to scale. At some point, you will need to decide what you can do that is most valuable to your business.

You might still be at a point in the growth of your business where you can be both in control and growing wealth.

There will come a time when you need to decide if the transition from founder to CEO is one that you want to make. Don't underestimate the change necessary for this transition, particularly if you have never been in a senior leadership role. But if you are the right person for this role, then do it! That's what's best for you and your business.

The alternative rich role will likely involve you focusing on tech, development, customer engagement, and raising wealth. So, while you're not the king, you will be doing work you love and that is best for your business.

Either way, doing the right work for you will help you be a legendary leader in your business.

Bullets and barrels

The analogy of bullets in (gun) barrels is very applicable here. You can go to battle with all the ammunition in the world, but your business will fail without any gun barrels to provide the direction. Some people can act as a gun barrel by directing others. Other people are really potent as bullets and will do a tremendous job in their area of expertise. If you're better as a bullet or wealth creator, then be that. And find the best barrel to direct the work in your business.

This part (Three) of the book will help you explore the work you must do and the work you love to do and ensure you do those. You will learn to let go and delegate where you're becoming a bottleneck and a liability. This will create a much smarter work environment for you and your whole team to thrive.

Do the right work

Given this may be your first time leading a business, how can you be expected to know what you should and shouldn't be doing? I imagine you don't want to handball work off to your team because they're already overworked. So who's going to do the work? You might need to get creative and open your thinking to new ways of working.

Doing the right work is not just about completing a list of tasks that you believe are the responsibility of a founder or CEO. It's about the essential work you do to help your business scale. This work is best done by you *because* you're the founder. It includes things like designing product features, meeting critical clients, or presenting at board meetings.

Founders often get caught up in the busyness of high growth, pace, band-aiding, and hiring. You don't take a step back and remember why you started your business in the first place. It might have been a passion project or a ground-breaking concept, yet sometimes you're not enjoying your work anymore. You're afraid of failure and disappointing people. Your vision has lost focus or is becoming out of reach. You're starting to feel like you're the only one who really cares.

In this chapter, we'll help you establish role clarity. We'll look at the work you must do. It can be a mix of work you love that you should Do and work you don't particularly enjoy that you should Develop.

We'll also look at the work you shouldn't do – the non-essential work that you need to Decrease or Delegate.

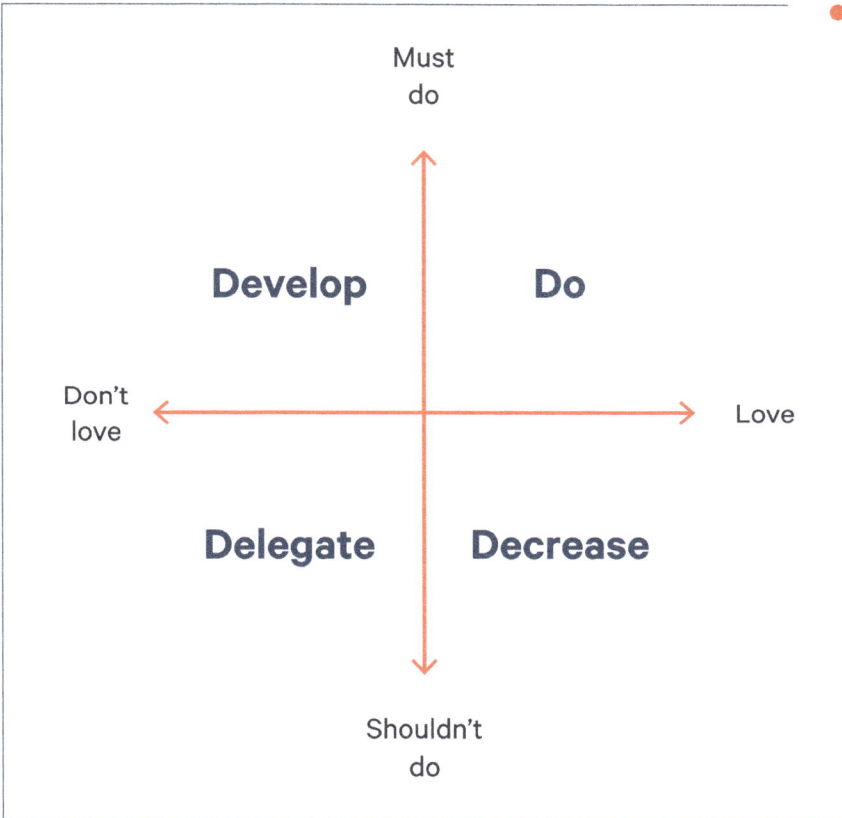

Model 5: Do the right work

Work you must do

Do

Do the legendary work. Recognise the work that you must do and that you also love to do.

If you are the designer of your product and need to take time out of the noise to be creative, generate ideas, and solve problems, do that.

If your strength is building customer relationships, get out and meet customers.

If you are the visionary for your business, the one who inspires the team, then get in front of them and inspire.

Develop

We all have to do work we don't love. It might be presenting to the board or taking part in panel discussions. It might be leading project meetings or having difficult performance conversations with your team. It might be fundraising, which is critical to your business.

Rather than avoid it, learn how to get better at it. You might learn to like it. Invest in developing your capability for this work.

Work you shouldn't do

Decrease

There will also be things you love doing that are no longer the role of the leader of a growing business. There will be technical challenges or marketing campaigns that you're eager to jump into, but it's not your place. Your team will already have a plan and know what they need to do, and you getting involved will likely cause a mess. Really.

I've often heard this situation described as 'the founder got involved, dropped a bomb, and walked off', leaving the team to work out who to take direction from and what approach they now need to take.

By all means, get involved at a strategic level in brainstorming challenges, leading innovative conversations or meeting with potential clients if that's what gives you energy.

But know when it's right to step away and let the people you hired to do this work get on with it.

Delegate

Delegate all the work that you consciously and intentionally must not do. It's the day-to-day stuff, like approving stationery orders, sourcing candidates online, doing first-round interviews, organising tech for new hires, updating org charts, and sending meeting invitations. Wait, are *you* a roadblock?

I know, you're being told to delegate, but everyone is busy.

Delegating to others in your team helps them to grow and develop. It shows you trust them, and it will help them feel engaged. If you keep everything to yourself, you alienate your team and your business won't be able to scale. There is great talent throughout your business – give them a chance.

FAIL TO SCALE BY FAILING TO LET GO

Fail to scale by failing to let go

'There's a time when they (founder) are the person to make it the best thing ever, but then they have to do this weird flip and become the best leader ever, and let go of a whole load of other stuff. Failing to let go is part of the reason a lot of startups never scale.'

– Dominic Price, Work Futurist, Atlassian[3]

In the simplest terms, the more time you spend doing work you shouldn't do, the more likely you are a liability to your business. Let go.

A legendary leader does the right work. It's the strategic work that only you should — and possibly only you can — do. You're the face of your business. You're the person the board wants to hear from. What you do and how you do it is seen and felt by everyone involved. How you lead your team has the greatest impact on the whole business.

Else, what's the point?

This may sound obvious, but I have worked with so many clients who have stuck with careers they truly hate. For example, one client created a solution that supports people's mental wellbeing. They have grown a business with amazing potential, but they are spending all their time solving operational issues as they arise. The solution they created was purpose-led, but now they are conflicted about how they fulfil that purpose. They're pretty miserable and are making everyone around them miserable too.

Dan Pink describes people's motivators and drivers as falling into three categories: autonomy, mastery and sense of purpose.[4]

Are you experiencing these in your role?

- Do you have autonomy in leading your business, or are you being pushed to make decisions that aren't aligned with your intentions?

- Are you achieving mastery in your work, or are you doing work that many other people could be doing?

- Do you feel a strong sense of purpose and meaning in your work, or has it lost that direction for you?

Doing a role that motivates you is really important. I regularly speak with founders in scaleups who meet the challenge of what to do. If you just want to code, then code. If you only want to develop product, then go and develop product. If you simply want to be an engineer, then be an engineer! You didn't grow this business not to do what you really want to do. What's the point of that? It's not all about sales, revenue, shares, building a team, impressing investors, and making money – especially if you're miserable! If you're miserable, you're likely being a liability.

THE
FOUNDER
IS PROBABLY
NOT THE
BEST CEO

You're probably
not the best CEO

A founder moving into the CEO role is not always the best option for the business. Recent movies have depicted the mess created by founders who took the wrong role.

WeCrashed[5] shows how WeWork's valuation fell from US$47bn in 2019 to US$2.9bn in 2020[6] under founder Adam Neumann's leadership. Similarly, in July 2016, Uber was valued at US$68bn, but its valuation dropped the following year to US$48bn.[7] In the movie *Super Pumped*,[8] we saw how founder Travis Kalanick's leadership was central to the devaluation and led to his forced resignation in 2017.

Not all founders who are CEOs of their own companies have been forced to resign from that position. There are many examples of founders who made that difficult but wise choice themselves. Kate Morris is no longer the CEO of Adore Beauty. Mia Freedman is not the CEO of Mamamia. Zoe Foster Blake is not the CEO of Go-To. Camilla Franks is not the CEO of Camilla. And Emily Weiss, founder of the American beauty company Glossier, stepped down in June 2022 after eight years as CEO.

The CEO role is critical to the success of your business. But know that it requires strong people leadership and a whole new set of skills. It is much more than a status position.

If you believe you will be a great CEO, then do that. If you need some help in becoming CEO, invest in that support and develop into the role. Whatever you do, don't assume you'll make the best CEO just because you're the founder. If you'd rather be the CPO or CTO or CMO, then be that.

As the founder, you can't completely avoid people leadership but if you're honestly not very good at it, then leave the CEO responsibility (and people leadership) to someone who is. That might be someone already in your team, or you can bring in the right person with the right experience and expertise for the job.

In his book *Play Nice But Win*, Michael Dell shares that one of the biggest mistakes he made early in his career was not hiring the right people around him.[9] At the age of twenty-one, he was growing his business, PCs Limited. There were no other founders, no venture capitalists or board of directors. He said, 'The management structure of PCs Limited was missing a crucial piece at the top. I needed someone with the kind of experience running a company that I didn't have.'

Don't be the CEO just because you think it's expected. You might be surprised to hear how often that's not the case. Advisors and boards can be hesitant to suggest to a founder that they step away from the CEO option, in case it creates curiosity in the market. Have the conversation. You will always be the founder — and that comes with its own set of responsibilities.

I recently spoke with Chris Tait, managing director at Henslow and non-executive chair at Atomos. He said, 'Very often, scaling the business becomes beyond the capability of the founder. The best founders realise this before it becomes an issue. They relinquish control and bring in the right talent, in particular a good 2IC (second in command), to help the founder bring their vision to life.' This is legendary leadership.

ESTABLISH
YOUR
BOUNDARIES

Establish your boundaries

Regardless of the role you take on in your business, establishing clear boundaries is essential for clarity. As a founder, you are used to doing everything. You find it hard to step away and let other people lead work in your business. Take the opportunity to establish boundaries, protect the work that needs to be done and enable your team to do the work they were hired to do.

The writer Jenée Desmond-Harris had this to say about how to divide your to-do list: 'I started dividing my to-do list into 1) things I have to do, 2) things I want to do, and 3) things other people want me to do. Life changing! I often don't get to #3 and I finally realized... this is what it means to have boundaries.'[10]

Once you have established your boundaries, communicate them clearly to your team, or else there will be confusion. Set clear expectations of who will pick up the work you're no longer doing, and set the boundaries for your team. Sometimes, your involvement is unavoidable, but this should be the exception.

Not just stepping on toes

Here's a scenario that might help shift your mindset and help create new boundaries.

Priceless

A founder and CEO I worked with had challenges with boundaries. Jenny needed to source some new engineers but didn't have a recruiter or P&C person to support the work. So she spent hours and hours trawling LinkedIn looking for potential candidates. She didn't necessarily love this work, but she did it because she knew what she was looking for. (Assuming no one else did....) We discussed this task.

? How many hours did Jenny spend just sourcing a candidate? 20 hours.

? How many hours in interviews? 6 hours.

? Approximately how much per hour is her time worth? She is taking an AU$200k salary, which is roughly $100 per hour.

The cost of Jenny doing this work added up to $2,600. And this was only the financial cost. It did not account for the time spent or the important work that was postponed or missed because her focus was elsewhere.

The business had recently recruited a superstar administration manager, Susie. We discussed delegating the online searches to her, with very clear criteria to support the work. The next time an engineer was needed:

- ✓ Susie did the online search, saving Jenny 20 hours.
- ✓ Jenny still did the interviews (which was fine).
- ✓ The admin person was on a contract rate of $35 per hour, so with 20 hours of work, that came to $700.
- ✓ The financial cost was $1,300, with a saving of $1,300. That's half the previous cost. The cost of freeing up 20 hours of the founder and CEO's time? Priceless.

Creating boundaries for yourself and allowing your team to do their work and have their own boundaries is more than not stepping on toes. It also has positive financial implications for your business.

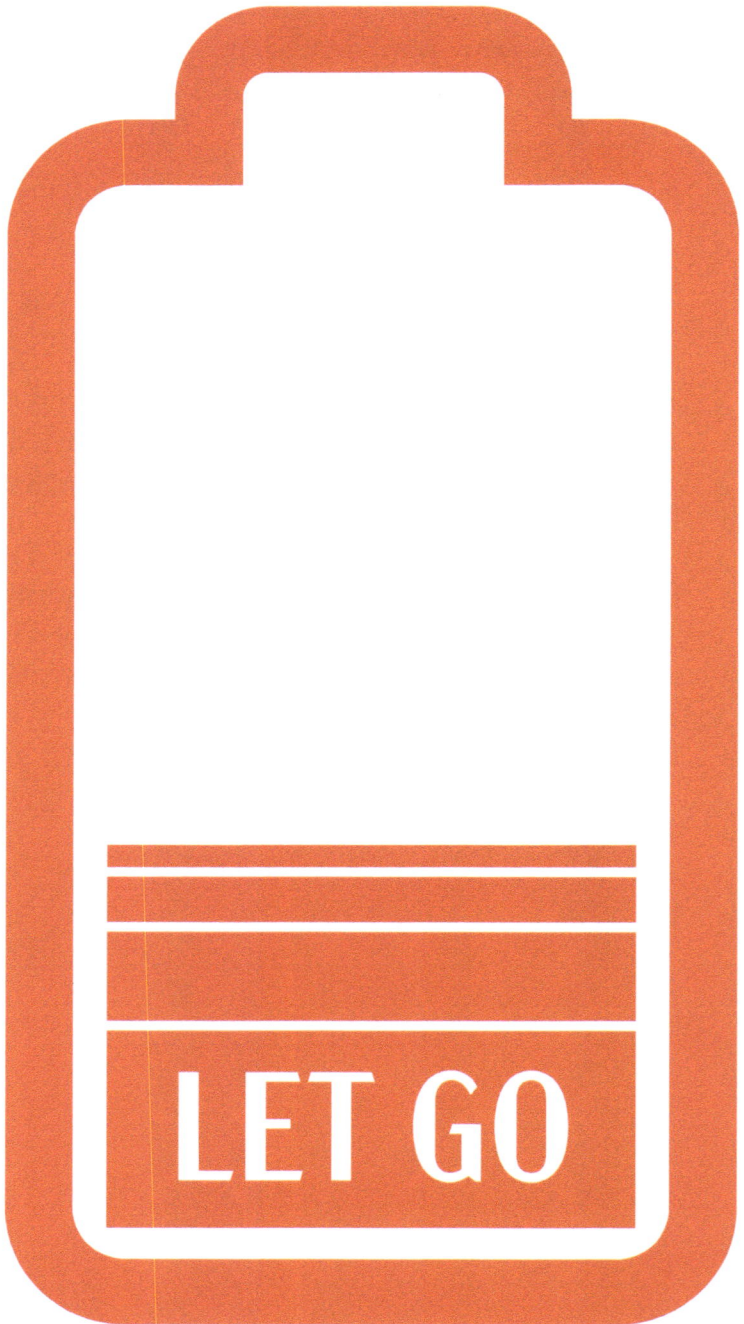

LET GO

Stop doing all the stuff

Is this you?

You do your best thinking first thing in the morning. You wake up rested and feeling fresh, energised about your day. You've got some critical work that must be done, and you make the space for just that. Or you had a great new idea yesterday, and want to think it through, make some notes and play with some concepts. Imagine. Create. Dream.

What actually happens...

You wake up, pick up your phone and check your emails with one eye still asleep. That sets the pattern for your morning. There have been some conversations online overnight, and you respond immediately. The issue might not be critical, but you want to address it before it escalates. You drag yourself out of bed because you worked late and didn't get enough sleep. You make a large coffee and settle in to reply to emails.

Before you know it, it's 10am. And all you've done is react to other people's needs! You have a sugar crash because you've been snacking on chocolate instead of making breakfast. You spend the rest of the day logging in to meeting after meeting, with the only 'working' time at the very end.... And so, the cycle of crazy continues.

That is not what you signed up for. It is making you feel stifled, irritated, frustrated, and exhausted. You have no time for family or friends. Your whole day is a series of distractions. You're working ridiculously hard but feel like you're getting nothing done. It shouldn't be like this. You're risking becoming a liability.

Jane Newton (Martino), consultant, advisor, investor, director, and co-founder of Smiling Mind, shared with me that founders need to separate out the things they need to change, although many don't like being told what to do. It's not a badge of honour to be sleepless and strung-out.

There are numerous activities and frameworks you can use to help you to break this bad work practice and learn to *let go*.

Here are some ideas:

✓ Use the 'do the right work' model to map out what you must and must not do. Identify the work you love to do, and do that.

✓ Read *Essentialism* by Greg McKeown. I recommend this book to all my clients. McKeown writes, 'Non-Essentialists tend to be so preoccupied with past successes and failures, as well as future challenges and opportunities, that they miss the present moment. They become distracted. Unfocused. They aren't really there. The way of the Essentialist is to tune into the present…. To focus on the things that are truly important – not yesterday or tomorrow, but right now.'[11]

✓ Jeff Weiner, the former CEO of LinkedIn, famously carved out 'nothing' time every day. These 30-90 minute blocks were his time for thinking, coaching and reflection. He created buffers for himself to process what needed to happen, get to know his team, or spend time on personal development. Legend!

✓ In his blog, James Clear writes, 'Before you ask, "What should I do today?" ask yourself, "What should I remove today?" Create the space you need to succeed.' If you want to shift your mindset, break bad habits, and create good habits, go no further than his book, *Atomic Habits*.[12] Listen to it as an audiobook on the way to anywhere.

Legend List

1   Use the 'do the right work' model to map out what you must and must not do.

2   Establish and communicate clear boundaries.

3   Set up your day to give you space to work in ways that are best for you and your business.

Part Four

Relationships

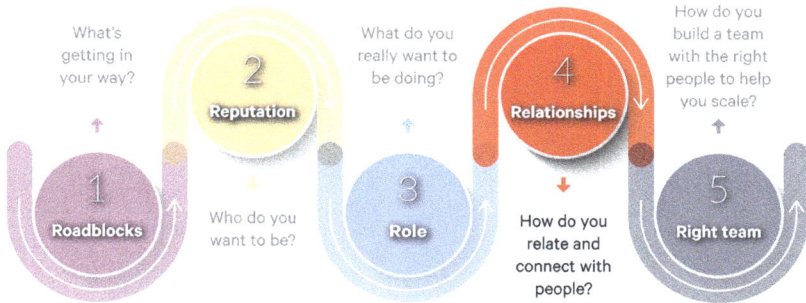

What's getting in your way?

1 Roadblocks

Who do you want to be?

2 Reputation

What do you really want to be doing?

3 Role

How do you relate and connect with people?

4 Relationships

How do you build a team with the right people to help you scale?

5 Right team

Who's got your back?

When it comes to scaling a business, the focus tends to be on the product, the tech, the go-to-market strategy, and the ARR (Annual Recurring Revenue). These are all very important, but you will struggle without the right people around you. Those who have your back.

Relationships take the shape of family, friends, co-founders, your leadership team, your broader team, the board, investors, customers, the market, and the whole ecosystem. Consider how you must foster each relationship to create a support infrastructure for you and your business.

Create an environment that involves a positive, healthy business culture where people are comfortable communicating, sharing ideas, working collaboratively, and providing effective feedback. A place where people connect. A community of people who will have your best interests in mind.

The following sections dive into these areas to provide insights into creating and growing the relationships you need as you scale.

Model 6: Understanding relationships

YOUR CULTURE IS YOUR BRAND

Your culture is your brand

It takes years for culture to be defined and established in a business, and it is constantly developing and evolving. It's like bodybuilding – you don't just lift weights once and expect a transformation. It requires regular, consistent work, stepping up the level of commitment as you grow until the new practices and behaviours are less conscious and become natural.

Describing your culture illustrates your company's brand. 'We're fun, committed, value-driven, and collaborative.' That's how people see your business.

Any inability to describe your company's culture implies to anyone watching or listening that the foundations are missing. And that suggests a level of chaos in your business. With the current global talent scarcity, your board and investors will want to see that you have a robust people and culture infrastructure to mitigate any risk of exposure.

Culture is your company's internal compass

Culture is how you behave. It's behaviours you actively promote and those you accept. It's about ways of working and how you interact with your team. It underlies communication, connection, diversity, leadership, teamwork, support, collaboration, action, results, drive, stability, and expectations.

You might not yet know what culture you want for your business, but make it a priority to work with your team to set an aspiration for your culture.

Particular industries (agritech, climate, AI, edtech, big data) automatically create a core culture. It is influenced by the people whose values align with working in that industry.

The culture is influenced by what's important to you and why you created this business. Your personal internal compass guides you to do what you do and how you do it. Similarly, the company's culture is its internal compass, just as Ben Horowitz says in the title of his book, *What You Do is Who You Are*.[1]

If you don't want a fun environment with chatty, sociable employees, don't try making it part of your culture. Many skilled employees seek an environment where they can put on their headphones and focus on deep, analytical work. If this is the case for your business, share it. That way, you will attract the behaviours you need, rather than trying to conform to some perceived recruitment expectation.

Be realistic. Know that what's meaningful to you may not be felt in the same way by your team. Of course, many people you hire will have similar values and purpose, but this job is often just a means to an end. You can, of course, influence their engagement. (More on this in Part Five.)

Your role as the founder strongly influences and shapes the culture. How you behave, communicate, connect, and lead sets the standard for everyone. Developing culture is your opportunity to create the environment and relationships you need to scale the business you want.

Culture is a business priority

Culture must be leader-led and leader-lived. Culture is not the responsibility of HR or People & Culture (despite the name). While everyone contributes to the culture in what behaviour is acted or accepted, the founder's role is to make the ultimate decisions about culture.

Company culture sets expectations for your business. Without a defined culture as an anchor, there is nothing to use as a reference for behaviour and supporting attraction, engagement and retention strategies.

In an HBR article, organisational psychologist Dr Rebecca Newton wrote that (culture) 'shapes the way people make decisions, get their work done, what they prioritize, and how they interact with colleagues, clients, and customers. It is really only successful and powerful when business leaders see it as their responsibility and see HR as a resource for helping them achieve it.'[2]

People must align with your company's culture and the standards of acceptable behaviour that you set.

Culture is not a policy

In their book, *Rework* (a must-read for any legendary leader), Jason Fried and David Heinemeier Hansson, founders of Basecamp, reason that we don't create culture — it develops over time. 'Culture is the by-product of behaviour. If you encourage people to share, then sharing will be built into your culture. If you reward trust, then trust will be built in.'[3]

I had a client who wanted help establishing a culture framework for her startup. We came up with some early concepts, and she said, 'Let's make that protocol. I need to develop a policy for that.' If you have a policy for your culture, you will have a policy culture. Just no!

We need to talk about onboarding

Onboarding is the first opportunity for your new hire to experience your company culture, aside from a tiny glimpse in the interview stage.

Information overload

You want your new hire to hit the ground running, but you also don't want to frighten them off on their first day. Be careful *not to overload them* with information or insist they meet the entire team as soon as they land.

And please, never have a planned team lunch on their first day. In, for example, the tech industry, how many people are extroverts who love meeting lots of new people in new environments and being the centre of attention? Yeah, not many. It's horrible, please don't do this.

Everyone should know that they each represent the brand and the business. Any new team member will want to see that everyone is excited about and invested in your product or service. Every interaction counts in developing these new relationships.

If you want the new hire to meet the function leads, then have some consistency and standard of information delivery. What does the new hire need to know? They only need to understand, at a high level, how each function collaborates with and impacts their role.

Use the following simple template I developed for leader introductions to new hires, with just three questions.

- What does your function do? Show them. Demo it.
- What does the new hire need to know – today?
- Who can they contact if they need help tomorrow?

That's it. Nothing else for now.

This is us

What do you remember about your first day in any job, the good and the bad? What would you like to have known on your first day? It could be as simple as finding out where the best coffee is.

Hopefully, your new hire will have had a positive experience before joining. Perhaps a branded pack of goodies was sent to their home, or everything is nicely placed on their desk when they arrive on day one.

Make anything a new hire can read about your company and their role available separately before they start.

Always have their tech set up and ready. This is non-negotiable.

Think about what they don't need on day one or that they'll forget in the overload of information. For example, how to submit expenses. Make that available separately, too, on a shared drive or the intranet.

Ensure the right person is leading the onboarding. It doesn't have to be their manager; it can be a person who does similar work to them and can show them the role. It's definitely not HR or P&C taking them through a bunch of slides.

The manager should be the first person they meet on day one and spend some allocated, quality time with them. An article for Gallup shared, 'When the manager takes an active role in onboarding, employees are 3.4 times as likely to feel like their onboarding process was successful.'[4]

As you grow, have an onboarding buddy system so people can continue to ask the 'silly questions'. The buddy can be anyone in the business, as these questions are often not job-specific.

Your availability might be limited, but meeting with the founder on the first day would be very exciting for most new hires. You might not get why, but trust me on this one. Make fifteen minutes available to say hi. It will have a huge impact.

Most importantly, make onboarding about the experience of your company. This is what it's like to work here. This is us.

YOU SET THE STANDARD FOR COMMUNICATION

You set the standard for communication

How often have you heard that 'communication is really bad here'? It can be quite frustrating. You're trying to get on with the work, but it feels like people in the team think they're entitled to know everything that's going on and should have input into every conversation.

As shared in the Roadblocks section, these are certainly signs that communication really is bad here. Here's what you might see:

- ✓ A lack of clarity of responsibilities and expectations.
- ✓ People are not enabled to do their jobs.
- ✓ Leaders don't communicate or are not transparent with what needs to be shared.
- ✓ Important information is lost or blocked.
- ✓ People are rattled by quick decisions that impact them.
- ✓ Teams are not included in decisions that impact them (where appropriate).

Those are serious challenges, all grouped under 'bad communication'. But what does communication mean?

Communication means different things

Communication means different things to different people. It might be about who needs to hear the information — the audience. For some, it's about the information or message that is shared. For others, it's about the delivery of that information, who delivers it and how. And for others still, it's about the channels of communication. It's the accessibility to information and the various mediums used to share it.

Communication involves four aspects.

1. The audience

Whatever you are communicating, first think about your audience. What do they need to hear, and how much detail? How will they receive and interpret your message? How do you position the message? What's in it for them? What do they value? What's happening in their world that might affect how they hear or respond to information? For example, are they already overloaded with work? Or are they silently in fear of being made redundant?

Different audiences need a tailored style and depth of message. For example, the leadership team may need to hear the context, the detail and the implications of a message. However, the development team might only need the high-level context and what the message or decision means for their team.

Since the pandemic, companies have had to adapt their communications to suit a remote workforce and ever-changing regulations. Whispir senior account executive Hilary Harrington shared with Business News Australia that we need to 'be more considered about what we're sending. How are we sending it? And what is the outcome we're trying to drive? And is this what will work best for the recipient as well?'[5]

2. The message

What you communicate is a big decision

What do people need to know versus what would they like to know? What should you share? People love to know what's going on. They want to know how it will affect them and their role. So, if it's not confidential, set up a way of ensuring they feel informed.

How much can you share?

Several years ago, I worked with a client where some key structural people changes were made. These decisions were based on confidential discussions with the board. If they had become public, they could have damaged the business's reputation and even caused an unnecessary loss of confidence. Know what you can and can't share, but let people know there are things you can't share. Silence creates rumours and speculation.

Consistency and clarity of messaging are imperative

Share the same message in the same way so that everyone hears the same thing. Be completely clear on what you want to share/your direction/your decision. If it's an important or sensitive business announcement, share it first with your leadership team. Check for clarity – have they received and interpreted the same message? Then share it with the broader team via relevant formats; say it, write it, repeat it, record it, post it.

Everyone hears messaging differently, so if you want to avoid negative reactions, set the standard for consistency and clarity of messaging. Consider too the real versus perceived urgency in sharing or responding to information.

3. The style of delivery

Your communication style typically relates to your delivery capability. This applies to one-to-ones, team meetings, all-hands, panel events, and board or investor presentations.

Stick to the point, don't overwhelm people with information and data. How often have you seen cringe-length death-by-PowerPoint decks with teeny writing and boring detail that no one wants to see?

Bring some energy. If the message is important, make it feel like it is.

If you don't like presenting publicly, get some help. It'll be worth it.

On occasion, get someone else to do the delivery, especially if they are the subject matter expert.

4. The channels of information

Poor channels of information can be easily amended through improved technology, the cadence of information flow and a skilled communications team. Make sure to set clear expectations and deliver regularly.

One of my P&C lead clients shared their frustration that they receive communication through many random channels. The CEO has a preferred platform, but rather than driving all communication through there, sometimes they send emails from any of many email addresses, or there might even be an occasional text. And the CEO gets annoyed if the team misses some information.

Companies like Poppulo, a global leader in employee communications technology, recommend a strategic omnichannel communications strategy. That means the engagement strategy is completely integrated with comms and tailored for the relevant employees wherever they work, on the channels and devices they prefer to receive, via the same platform.

If you want people to use one platform, drive everything through there. If you're afraid of people missing out, that's their issue. You set the standard, but please be consistent.

Being responsible for the culture of communication in your business is important. You cannot delegate this responsibility to anyone else. How you communicate greatly impacts how your team communicates and works together. Again, you set the standard.

Do you wing conversations?

We've all experienced situations where someone just starts talking *at* us. It can be confronting and confusing. Sometimes it involves emotion, and there appears to be no context to the information. You're left wondering what they want from you.

People like to know what's expected of them in any conversation. To get the most from the conversation, set the context and expectations early.

A conversation should never be based on hearsay or second-hand information. And any feedback (positive or constructive) or discussion should include examples. Different situations require different levels of preparation, but you will always achieve a better result if you do some groundwork. It shows respect to the other person too.

To build connection, hold the scheduled catchup with high importance. Be conscious of how often you postpone catching up with your team member. Or how often you might be running late, rushing or unprepared. What message does this give them?

Effective conversations

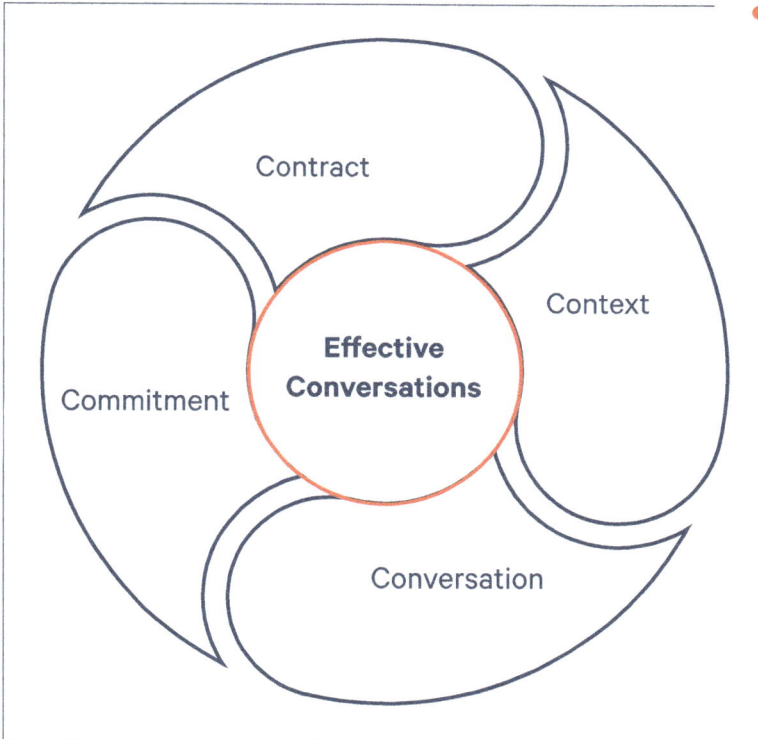

Model 7: Effective conversations

The expressions 'I have feedback for you' and 'We need to talk' have a visceral reaction for many people. Where possible, let someone know in advance what the meeting is about — without creating anxiety.

If the meeting is about a performance issue, consider how to let them know, gently. You don't want them to lose sleep or get anxious. If the meeting is just a casual check-in, then say that. Set the expectation.

Four things to remember to have an effective conversation:

1. Contract

Sometimes you might call someone or set up a meeting to vent or offload. Or you might just need a quick answer. You might be looking for coaching through an issue, or it might be a brainstorm.

Share your expectations clearly, either before or early in the conversation. 'I just want to share this information with you. I don't need anything from you today, just keep this information in mind when you're working on that project.' Equally, at any point, you can/should ask, 'What do you need from me in this conversation?'

2. Context

Where possible, share in advance why you're having this conversation. It might be, 'I'd like to run this past you before I head into the leadership team meeting today. We will be making decisions on the marketing team structure, and I just want to make sure I have all the correct information.'

Context is even more important if it's a difficult conversation. 'Today I'd like to focus on...so that we can.... Is that good with you? Is there anything else you'd like to discuss?'

3. Conversation

Develop the art of conversation. Listen, hear, ask clarifying questions, be present and engaged, and not distracted. Most importantly, remember that dialogue means it's two-way.

4. Commitment

Be really clear (at the start and throughout) about the expected outcomes from the conversation. It's often good practice to ask the other person to share what they believe are the action items, to know you are aligned. Sometimes it's necessary to follow up.

I had a manager who thought as she spoke and formed her ideas in the moment. At the next meeting, it would be clear that she had no recollection of the conversation or would say, 'That was just an idea; we're not going with it'. I learned to send her an email afterwards with 'Here's what I heard and what I believe we agreed on. Can you please confirm before I start working on this?' It saved me so much time, frustration, and wasted effort.

You might need to loop around and reclarify as you go. Expectations and roles change as the conversation progresses. Be prepared to reset them.

DELIVER

COMMUNICATION

CREATE

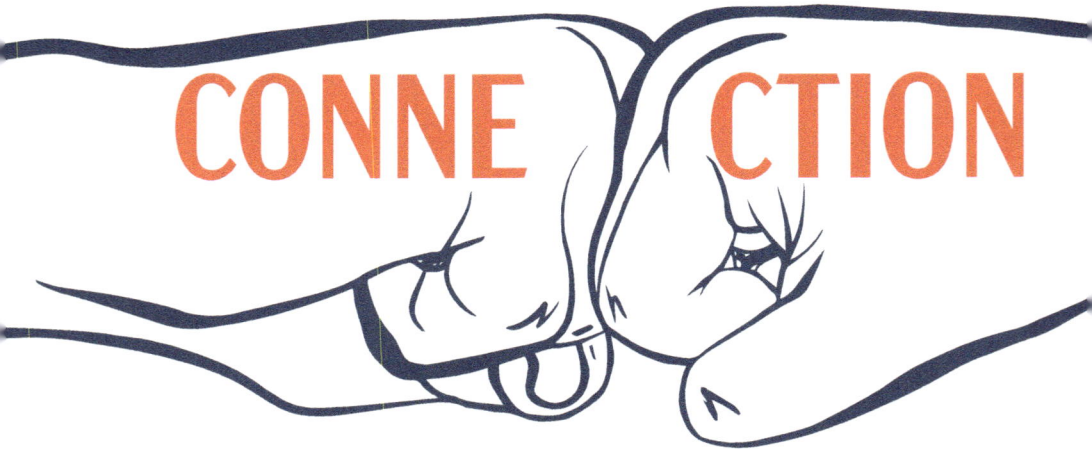

CONNE CTION

Create connection

Deliver communication, create connection.

As shared in this book, communication is about the audience, the message, the style of delivery, and the channels of information.

Connection is about creating alignment, responses, feedback, listening, questions, understanding, and clarification. It's creating a link between people, through shared work, values, purpose, thinking, and relationships. Building connection involves a high degree of trust – from both sides. Trust is built through transparency and honesty.

Linking to a common vision

Creating connection with your team is critical to your success as a legendary leader. If you speak *at* people and don't take time to listen and ask questions, they will feel disconnected and alienated. Connection with your team is critical to linking everyone to a common purpose or vision. Everyone must be speaking a common language and relating to each other.

Creating a strong connection with the people in your team builds a positive culture. It lifts engagement and retention and enables people to share their concerns safely. It allows people to share their aspirations for themselves and your business.

Take off your headphones

Moving to remote work has made connecting far more difficult in recent years. We missed the social cues and the nuances of connecting in person. Opportunities for incidental conversations in the hallways or while grabbing a coffee disappeared overnight. That is why focusing on making a connection is more important than ever. And it is taking a lot more effort.

But developing a connection doesn't need to be through a formal meeting or at an arranged time. Even with remote working, connections can still be maintained through quick conversations while waiting for others to join the video call, via a phone conversation (remember them?), or through the multitude of tech platforms available, such as Slack, Teams, or WhatsApp.

As the leader, know how much connection each person likes. Even if you prefer to work silently, with headphones on, or you like regular, personal interaction, each of your team will have their preference. Meet them halfway. Some will want to check in with you once every few days, while others might like you to contact them with a regular 'Good morning, how are you today? What's going on with you?' Find out what each person prefers. Just ask them.

But there's no time...

I often hear leaders saying they haven't time to speak to each team member. I believe they can't afford not to. It doesn't have to be anything intensive. If you're in the office, you can grab a coffee together or go for a 'walk and talk'. This is often a good option when the conversation can be difficult, as you're not facing each other.

Have a video lunch with your team on occasion. Or just check in with a quick 'How are you doing today?'

A simple format you can use is asking, 'What's on your plate? And how can I help?' The more often you ask, the shorter the conversation needs to be. No more than a couple of minutes. Everyone has time for this.

Make sure your team understands why you want to speak with them. They might be cautious or nervous if you're starting to increase connection. 'Why are they asking me this, now? What have I done?' It won't take long for this to become a habit but appreciate that there might be apprehension at first.

Connect with them to keep them

While informal checks-in and catchups support day-to-day operations, individuals should expect more formal, scheduled conversations about every three months. These conversations aim to review outcomes, workload, challenges, opportunities, careers, and development progress.

Far too often, leaders assume that people are happy in their roles. Just because someone doesn't come to share everything that's going on doesn't mean they're happy or not looking elsewhere for work. It's particularly relevant now that there is a talent scarcity, and people have more options for work elsewhere. Increased salary alone is not enough to retain talent.

Legendary leaders regularly check in with the team, as there are so many benefits to the individual and the business. There will be no surprises and less need for formal performance discussions and difficult conversations. With an increased level of trust, people will feel safe sharing what's going on.

They will more easily discuss opportunities for development and progression. It will be easier to identify future leaders. People will be recognised for their contribution, be more engaged, and naturally work better together. There will be greater alignment to deliver your strategy, with a stronger focus on the vision.

BEWARE
ALIGNMENT

D R I F T

Beware alignment drift

Successfully scaling your business requires foundational alignment among the co-founders and the leadership team. When you're not aligned, you waste time and money working in opposition – not to mention the frustration and tension that creeps in. As tension increases, alignment decreases.

While not always clearly defined from day one, you and your team generally do understand what you're working towards. Alongside the design and development of your product or service, these are the main areas of alignment:

Core purpose: Why are we here?

Vision: What do we aspire to achieve?

Values: What is important to us?

Reputation: What do we want to be known for?

Something's not right

Startups fail because of a lack of integration and alignment between the founders and within the leadership team. When you start your business, you're aligned. You know this because you discuss it. Regular early conversations confirm what you want from your business and how you will get there.

As your business grows, your beliefs, understanding, assumptions, and aspirations can drift apart. It can happen gradually and only become apparent when frustrations show up and decisions become difficult. You know something's not right, but either you haven't time to address it, or you hope things will work themselves out. Bad move.

The thing is never the thing

Sadly, I've seen actions and assumptions that have gone too far to bring co-founders or the leadership team back into alignment. Decisions have been made independently or against the advice of one party. The team starts taking sides. Alignment is often irredeemable.

As soon as you feel alignment is drifting, make a call. Get your co-founder and/or leadership team together to review and reset. I recommend getting external support to bring a neutral, unbiased perspective. It's far better for your business to make a call early than to let differences fester. There's more at stake than just you and your opinions (and ego).

When leaders become misaligned

Last year, I was engaged to work with a scaleup that was going through a major transition and likely to be exiting within months. I was briefed that Jason, a valued member of the senior leadership team, had become disengaged.

The founder was finding him difficult to manage. He wasn't collaborating and was losing visibility in the business. His peers felt he was becoming too independent, and they were losing access to his innovative contributions. The assumption was that he had just lost interest.

I met with Jason to uncover what was causing this shift in behaviour.

The truth for Jason was that he felt he was losing his place in the inner circle. He was unsure of his future with the business. His confidence was eroding, and he struggled to find his way back. The toughest part for him was that he was one of the original crew. He'd been there at the start, working the long days and nights, creating something brilliant. But now, he found all that connection and sense of accomplishment slipping away from him.

Once we started to lift the lid on what was going on for Jason, he took the space to step back, reset, and consider what he wanted for his future. We took action to rebuild Jason's confidence, his relationships with the founder and his peers, and his reputation in the business.

When things are moving fast and alignment is slipping, assumptions are the easiest path. We can miss what's going on beneath the surface. We must create space to uncover what's truly going on, then reset and realign.

CREATE YOUR

COMMUNITY

Your community has your back

To scale, you will need different people for different purposes. Your relationship with each group of people will be different. And how you lead in each situation will vary. Besides your close family and friends, the most important people in your community are your co-founder and peers, your team, the board and advisors, customers, suppliers, and the startup ecosystem.

Create your community

You can't do this alone. As a legendary leader, building a network or community around you requires you to keep your ego out of the way. Recognise that you need people, and each different relationship is essential to your success and that of your business.

By creating a community of people, you will have people to give you advice and direction, and provide support and expertise when needed. They will provide support for your vision and help you deliver that vision. These are the people who can help you get unstuck while respecting your boundaries. They have your back.

Get a mentor and coach

Other key support relationships I strongly recommend are a business mentor and a development or executive coach.

Typically, a business mentor can help you make the right, informed business decisions. They get your business, and they get you.

A coach can help you grow and develop as a legendary leader and help prevent you from becoming a liability to your business. Some people are cautious about a one-to-one coaching arrangement, and I can't tell you how often I've been told, 'I don't want any of that fluffy, kumbaya rubbish'. By this, I presume they don't want personal and professional development to become more a successful leader in their own business. *eye roll

What am I missing?

Zac Duff, co-founder and CEO of JigSpace, is a thinker. He likes to understand why and how things work. I mentioned earlier that Zac wants to be known for 'being fun to work with and making dope shit'.

Zac knew he was growing an incredible business. Still, he wanted to learn how to lift his leadership capability to the next level to best support his team (legendary leader right there). He engaged me as his coach through my *Legendary Leader* 90-day coaching program.

Every couple of weeks, we would meet to discuss what was happening for Zac, what changes he'd been making to think differently as a leader, and how he was adapting his leadership style to create the best culture for JigSpace.

Zac recently mentioned that the one piece of advice he keeps coming back to is asking himself, 'What am I missing?' This question arose so often in our conversations that now it's his first thought when faced with a challenge or an opportunity.

You can use this tool to raise questions in any interaction.

? When someone isn't delivering as discussed: Did I share my expectations clearly?

? When someone oversteps the boundaries: Do they have role clarity?

? When someone behaves unexpectedly: What was their true intention?

? When the board makes a request that you don't like: Why are they really asking for this?

? When a customer challenges a product feature: Is this valid?

? When someone has an idea you don't like: What's the opportunity I'm not seeing?

? When it seems like you're speaking different languages: How can I help them hear me?

? To better communicate and connect with each person in your community, always ask yourself, 'What am I missing?'.

Legend List

1 Culture is leader-led and leader-lived. It's not a set of values on the wall.

2 Preparing for any conversation guarantees a far better outcome for everyone.

3 Build connections with your community; you never know when you'll need them.

Part Five

The Right Team

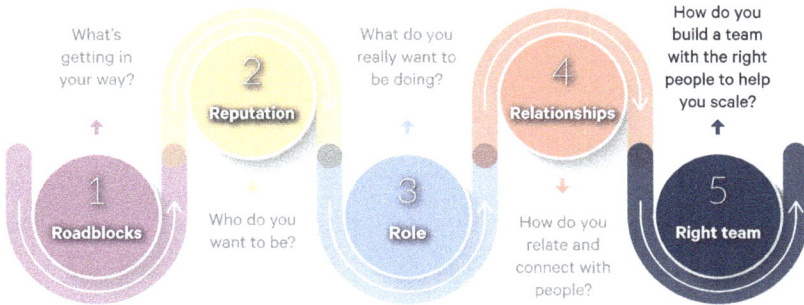

What's getting in your way?

1 Roadblocks

2 Reputation

Who do you want to be?

What do you really want to be doing?

3 Role

4 Relationships

How do you relate and connect with people?

How do you build a team with the right people to help you scale?

5 Right team

Choose right

Having the right team is when you have the right people in the right place with the right capability, experience and attitude, with the people infrastructure and frameworks to support them.

The people with the right capability and experience have relevant expertise to suit the current and (near) future role requirements. Here, we also encourage decisions about what to do with those people whose capability has reached its ceiling or were hired beyond the need for the role.

Attitude is an important part of the behaviour and attributes that align with your company culture and values, such as teamwork, respect, quality, focus, and ambition. When a company scales and people's roles and responsibilities change, some can become disgruntled or feel they're no longer part of the inner circle. This can be disruptive to the rest of the team.

Building the right team takes regular attention.

Value people

I wince whenever I hear the expression 'people are our greatest asset'. Of course, they should be, but they are rarely seen this way. If people are truly your greatest asset, show me your budget allocation to attracting, developing, engaging, and retaining them. Aha, just as I thought. There is often no budget for people development. And in challenging times, it is always the first thing to go. Always. Just when you need people to be able to step up and drag your business out of a mess, you take away the one thing that's keeping them up. It's like taking away the ladder.

The easier part of creating the right team is having conversations on performance discussions, attraction and retention strategies, and career paths. However, these will become irrelevant and merely frustrating if frameworks and infrastructure aren't in place for people to develop as your business grows. It will all feel like lip service.

People infrastructure is the support for any part of the employee lifecycle (from joining your business to exiting), such as engagement surveys with action plans, leadership development programs, learning management systems, and succession plans. This may sound overwhelming, but this chapter will help you use a simple process to identify what you need.

THE
RIGHT
PEOPLE
IN THE
RIGHT
PLACE
WITH THE
RIGHT
CAPABILITY
EXPERIENCE
AND
ATTITUDE

Review your team structure

We've all seen the videos of little kids playing on a football pitch. It's crazy out there. There is no order, no one knows what they're supposed to be doing, everyone's charging after the ball, and no goals are scored. And to make it worse, parents yell instructions from the sidelines. It's a total cluster. Hilarious, but a cluster.

It's not so hilarious when this is your business. Is this happening for you? Is everyone running around like clueless kids or headless chooks? Are they looking to you for direction but instead are getting yelled at from the sidelines?

If you're wondering about it, then it's probably the right time for a team structure review.

As your business grows, your business strategy changes and a redesign enables you to move to the next stage. Think about your team as the kids on the pitch.

Prevent the crazy

Working with a fast-growing client, that was how it was starting to feel for everyone in the team. I was engaged to help review and redesign the team, capturing the points where this team was no longer working.

The founder/CEO was at a loss. He believed he was communicating well with the team, but he was more like the parent on the sideline, creating more confusion and being eternally disappointed.

As the business was growing quickly, new people challenges started to appear. The existing team no longer knew the boundaries, or even who these new employees were. The newbies didn't know where they fit either. Everyone was starting to grab their territory.

Business requirements had outgrown current capabilities. Some of the people who had helped bring success to the business were no longer capable of building the future. Some had limited capability, which was fine until it started to become an issue when they couldn't deliver as needed.

Some people who enjoyed the uncertainty of a startup environment were not suited to the new environment where process, guidelines, and policies were introduced. Some of them recognised they no longer fit, and they left. Others became disgruntled, causing upset among the team.

Hierarchies were naturally forming as growing numbers of people needed a manager. Some people found themselves in management roles without the skills to manage or lead people. This led to mismanaged expectations, damaged relationships, and poor business results.

Most people started questioning their future roles in the business. They wanted to know about career paths, pay reviews, and promotions. They needed clarity, and they needed capability frameworks to reference in conversations.

You can imagine the negative impact of all this on the culture. It was directly responsible for the loss of several key employees.

Gathering the leadership team, we worked through a four-phased process to review and redesign the team structure.

Worth the effort

Reviewing your team and the supporting people infrastructure will raise some necessary changes. It can feel like a lot of work, but it's worth it. The benefits to the business and the team outweigh the effort.

Here's one example of how the benefits to the business and the team outweigh the effort. I worked with Paul Naphtali, (co-founder and managing partner, Rampersand VC) and his team over several months on a team review. Paul said, 'My team were asking for job descriptions, but I hadn't realised how this all interlinks. Now I have the right team, and each person has exactly what they need – relevant job descriptions, support for career conversations, development action plans and clear promotion paths. It is absolutely worth the effort to do this right!'

As you scale, your business can deliver towards the future business strategy rather than rest on today's requirements. It ensures you have the right people in place today and identifies those future leaders to be developed and ready to step up when needed. This initiative provides visibility of who is in your business and what talent they have, identifying any capability and diversity gaps that need to be addressed.

Implementing a succession framework mitigates risk for your business of any single-point sensitive capability, such as an individual with a unique technical skill. It helps to support attraction and retention strategies and gets in front of any risk of people considering leaving. It builds your competitive advantage.

The process improves team engagement by providing a reference framework they can use to share their aspirations and for performance and development conversations. It's an opportunity to create a learning and development infrastructure with defined career paths, and can be used to build relevant and useful job descriptions.

Once you have reviewed your team, it is time for the redesign – making those necessary changes, having difficult conversations, investing in development, and implementing the infrastructure to support the changes.

The four phases of team structure review

Most businesses start at the wrong end of this process. They hire to fill role gaps or organically grow the teams as the business grows. Alex leaves, and they hire Alex 2.0 without taking an holistic view of what's changed since Alex was hired. How much has the business grown? Are those same skills still needed? How successful was Alex in that role? Did they have the necessary skills? What else could they have taken on? Who else in the team has moved or been replaced that impacts the role?

The problem here is that a short-term solution will not enable your business to scale. You will end up with the wrong team and people who cannot scale with you.

We discussed role clarity for the founder and CEO in Part Three: Role. Establishing role clarity across the entire team is imperative to enable your business to scale. In my experience, lack of role clarity is the biggest roadblock to scale.

There are four phases to reviewing your team to design a new scalable team structure.

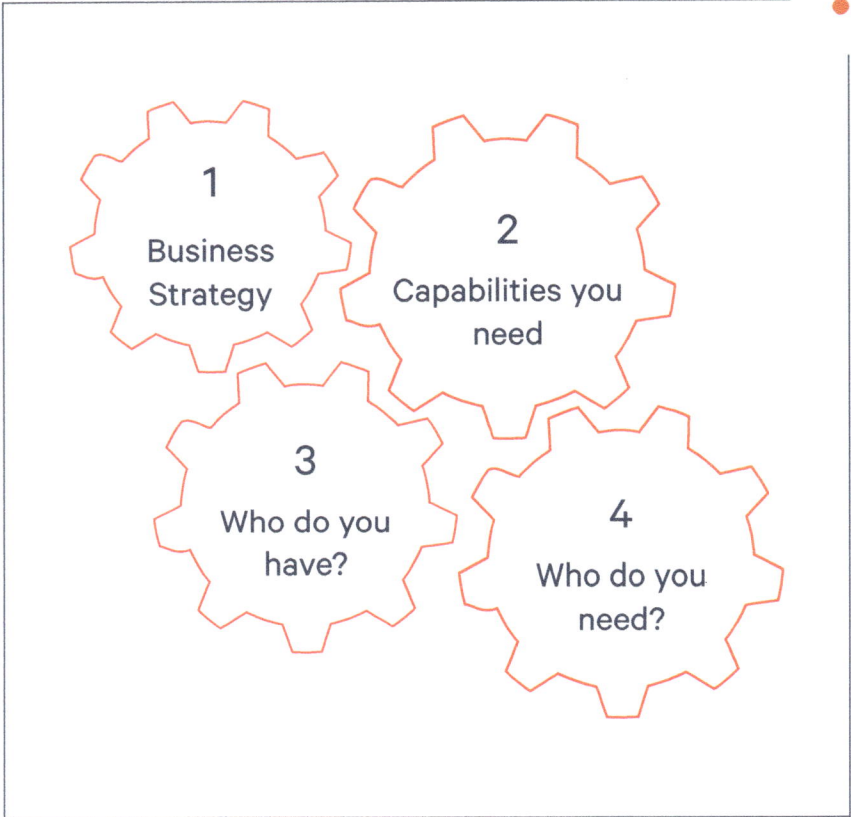

Model 8: Review your team structure

I strongly recommend that you don't try this without the support of someone with expertise in organisation design. It's tricky and can involve emotional decisions. You can't afford to get this wrong.

Let's look at each of these phases in turn.

Phase One: What is your business strategy?

We start with a clear business strategy and consider how this will impact your team review.

What is your current strategy? What are your plans for the next six to twelve months and one to three years? (If you can extend that far out.)

Here are some questions to consider from a people perspective, at both business and team or functional levels.

- What are your business goals, and how will you measure success?

- What are the biggest challenges you're facing today as you lead your business?

- What are your three key strengths compared with your competitors?

Phase Two: What capabilities do you need?

This activity requires going back to basics.

Take a blank sheet of paper or a screen, and imagine you have no current employees. I know this can be hard – but try it. Our decisions are too easily biased by thinking about the people we already work with.

What capabilities are needed to meet your current and future business strategy requirements? Consider both behavioural/ qualities and technical/function-specific capabilities.

Some questions to consider:

- What is your rationale for your current structure?
- What people or capabilities changes might accelerate meeting your goals?
- Do you have the capabilities now, or can you hire and train for them?

Developing capability frameworks

Often team structures form organically. You have likely back-filled urgent gaps, replacing the same people into the same roles rather than understanding what capabilities are really needed. Instead, I recommend creating a capability framework for your business. It doesn't have to be complex, but it must be live and evolving.

A capability framework provides consistent and credible titles for reference and measure. It's also an essential element of any hiring plan. As a new business grows, some very interesting titles emerge. You can use whatever naming format works internally, but it's important to be able to say 'this is similar to a senior manager level role' – something the market recognises. For example, head of HR = People & Culture lead = head of People and Engagement.

Another element is the alignment of levels. You probably won't want hierarchies and reporting lines, but your team needs them. Knowing where they fit, who they report to, who is responsible and who makes the decisions will help prevent much tension and frustration. Again, it doesn't mean matching titles throughout the business, but aligning levels is key for career path and remuneration purposes.

You will need two capability frameworks.

1. Technical capability framework

For each capability, create a high-level list of technical skills and activities required to meet the strategy. Capability categories for your sales function might include Market, Events, Forecasting, and New opportunities.

These can each be broken down into sub-capabilities as needed. For example, Market could be: grow the brand, know the market, grow the market.

You can break this down further by developing descriptions for each of these, for each possible level of the role.

2. Behavioural or qualities capability framework

While the technical capability framework is *what* you do, the behavioural capability framework defines *how* you deliver the strategy.

The behavioural capability framework is designed to identify the qualities, traits, and behaviours needed in your employees to align with your culture. This might include developing the right team, driving results, and leading collaboratively. Include your company values in this framework.

Like technical capabilities, these can be broken down further, for example, by core and leadership capabilities.

Phase Three: Who do you have?

Now you are clearer on the capabilities necessary to meet your business strategy requirements, and have capabilities frameworks to support any conversation or decision on what you need. The next step is to look at who is on your existing team.

Some questions to consider:

? Who of your existing employees meet the strategy requirements?

? How do they map onto each of the capabilities frameworks?

? Where are the capability gaps in your business?

Mapping your existing team to the frameworks

There are two steps here:

1. Using each framework as a reference, consider where each person has capabilities. For example, they may be strong at 'Leads collaboratively' but need development in 'Delivers results'.
2. Consider their ability, engagement and aspirations with your business.

? Ability: Can they do their job? How well do they perform?

? Engagement: Do they strongly believe in your goals and vision? Are they willing to go above and beyond to help your business to scale?

? Aspirations: What would they like to be doing in one to three years? Are they willing to take on additional work to accelerate their growth?

This is best achieved through conversations with each person, particularly about their aspirations, as assumptions about people's future are often incorrect.

Another important topic for discussion with your leadership team is who in their teams might be considering leaving the business. Again, making assumptions here can be devastatingly wrong.

What would be the impact of that person leaving? If their skills are difficult to replace in the marketplace, promptly invest time, energy, money, and effort in retaining them. To mitigate the risk to the business, identify and develop a successor who can do their work if they do choose to leave. Don't wait until it's too late.

Phase Four: Who do you need?

Failing to let go is part of why many startups never scale, says Dominic Price, Work Futurist, Atlassian. But the way to counter that is to hire people you can trust and who can do certain aspects of the business even better than the founder.[1]

Now that you understand the capabilities within your business and the aspirations of the people supporting you to deliver your strategy, how can you support their development? With this in mind, it's time to establish (what and) who you need.

The right 'who you need' is a combination of technical capability and (of course) behavioural capability that aligns with your culture.

Design your new team structure

It's important to remember that none of this is set in stone. At the growth stages, everything is evolving and up for constant review. Try it out, and see what works best for you.

Some questions to consider:

- What does the new team structure look like with the existing team in place?
- Where are the priorities for new roles, promotions, hiring?
- What can you do today to start to fill the gaps?

Parting ways

Some people might no longer fit this new structure. Their skills may have become obsolete, their responsibilities may be combined into another role, and their behaviours may no longer suit the culture you have built for your future. It may be time for a cleanout, to have tough conversations with these people. You may be able to redeploy them, but you may also need to part ways.

Filling the gaps

The capability infrastructure design should involve managers/ leaders having regular conversations with existing team members about their performance. The purpose is to develop capabilities through short and longer-term development opportunities, such as setting stretch goals, leveraging inter-team projects, and attending conferences.

For position gaps, consider where the holes are in your new structure. Where are the capability gaps you cannot fill internally, even with training and development? What are some of the people leadership roles you can develop or bring into your business?

How do you build all of this into your recruitment process?

FILL

THE

GAPS

Where's my job description?

Employees often request a job description. Am I right? This is usually about them wanting to understand what's expected of them and where they fit in the organisation.

Job descriptions are like recipes. They're detailed and specific. You need a certain number of ingredients, with a particular measure, added at the right time and in the right proportions. Sure, there's an opportunity to substitute products that are not currently available, but it's not ideal. We apply a recipe for a purpose; because, through time and testing, we've learned this is what works best.

With a global talent scarcity, clear and relevant job descriptions have become even more critical.

Here's a warning, though. Most job descriptions are written with the incumbent in mind. They fail to reflect the capabilities, experience, and behaviours needed to execute the future business strategy. They are often not useful or current because businesses tend to start at the last step of a good hiring process, asking 'Who do we need?'. They backfill or replace like with like. Remember? Alex left, so you hired Alex 2.0.

This 'right team' process involves developing a more in-depth review of your business and team structure, but the outcome is that you hire the right team for your business. As a bonus, you get clear and easily-populated job descriptions for current and future requirements.

Hopefully, you can now see that you and your team have clarity of roles, responsibilities, capabilities (technical and behavioural), career paths, capability gaps, future leadership potential, and bench strength leading to success.

The final piece is to use all this information to quickly and accurately develop job descriptions for existing and new roles. It's a simple exercise of populating the JD from the available frameworks.

Expertise

What technical capabilities can you take from the framework at the relevant level? The desired qualifications will also be clear, particularly any new expertise not currently in the business.

Experience

You will know how many years of experience are needed to do the work at that level and what relevant experience is essential (people manager, the particular industry, cultural awareness).

Qualities

Behavioural capabilities can be selected to describe the qualities and traits at the level of the person you need, aligning with the business culture and values.

What else?

If you can implement the four phases of building the right team, your business will be in a strong position to scale from a people structure perspective. You have identified the changes that need to happen, and now you must implement them.

Now you've mapped your business strategy to your people strategy (capabilities, who you have, who you need) and have all the right processes in place to build this infrastructure. There's still plenty of hard work to do to fill the gaps properly and create and retain the right team.

As a founder, you must learn to let go and trust your team to grow your business. There will be team members who do not fit your vision of the future for your business or have the capability to step up, and it's time to let them go.

Hire the right people (you now know their profile), not just the smartest people. While doing this, figure out how to avoid the many costly and common hiring mistakes.

Establish the frameworks to ensure your team continues to grow and develop. Share your vision with the world through an effective employee value proposition. Develop a strong engagement strategy to retain the right people in your business.

We'll discuss how you can do this in the following chapters.

Letting go, the right way

An individual's lack of role clarity is compounded when they are part of a leadership team whose role clarity is unclear. Defining the role of your leadership team early will help ensure you have the right people in the room, with the clarity and capability to do the right work and make the right decisions. They will learn to communicate effectively and create a culture that embraces role clarity.

Stepping out

A recent client, RIchard Wyles of Totara Learning in Wellington, NZ, wanted my support in assessing the effectiveness of his senior leadership team (SLT), understanding the impact of this team's role, and identifying and addressing recommended improvements.

I met with Richard and the head of P&C to understand our starting point so we could establish what we wanted from the SLT and what roles each member would play. To support this, I met with each SLT member individually. Our discussion ranged across what was working well, what they could be doing differently, what was holding the team back, and what success looked like. While there were similarities in their comments, there were some clear differences too.

We identified influences that had challenged the business through its recent high growth. These included the global pandemic, recent unexpected loss of key talent, raised candidate expectations due to talent scarcity, a mix of new and older team members, and varying levels of leadership capability. Overall, they felt there were low reserves due to the high growth.

The key deliverables required were frameworks and tools for the team to work more effectively with actionable outcomes. The leaders were asked to step up and hold themselves to account, improve communication across the silos, and develop trust and engagement as an SLT. Alignment of the team to the company's vision and values also needed to be addressed.

On the positive side, the SLT were willing and eager for things to improve. They recognised that each person brought strengths and wanted to learn how to best leverage them to benefit the whole team. There was a desire to grow, learn, and align their efforts to build a high-performing SLT.

We established that improvements needed for the SLT to be more effective fell into four categories.

Clarity: They needed to define what it meant to be an SLT member. What work needed to be done? Who was accountable for what?

Capability: Were the right people in the room? We questioned the imbalance of experience and expertise of SLT members. There was a mix of tenured members and those who'd come in from larger corporate environments; each with different capabilities and expectations of an SLT.

Communication: Communication is central to the effectiveness of the senior leadership team. There were many roadblocks to clear communication, including distributed teams, a tendency toward operating in silos and each leader's varied communication style.

Culture: This was the biggest opportunity for improvement. It involved reviewing the alignment and engagement of the team. Different leadership styles meant a broad range of engagement differences.

To address these challenges, we agreed on a series of team workshops and individual executive coaching sessions. These sessions were to lift capability, establish consistent, acceptable ways of working, and drive a positive culture within the SLT. These improvements could then be embedded across the business.

Without role clarity for individual members and the SLT as a team, it would be impossible for the SLT to become high performing.

STOP TOLERATING BRILLIANT JERKS

Let them go

One bad employee can destroy company culture. Far too often I see clients tolerating bad attitudes and behaviour – including from the leadership team. By protecting and accommodating these people (they are liabilities) and trying not to upset them, you may be missing the fact that tolerating this behaviour can be detrimental to the broader team. The behaviours you accept, both good and bad, set the standard for the whole business.

In high-growth businesses, there are two main situations where poor behaviours are allowed to continue and potentially destroy your business.

Stop tolerating 'brilliant jerks'

Brilliant jerks are technically talented people who display unfavourable behaviours that can be disruptive and even distressing to others. Allowing them to continue to behave this way can destroy any attempts by the broader team to live by the company values and align with the culture you're trying to build. Addressing the challenges of these employees, while difficult, is crucial.

In 2019, Atlassian addressed the issue of 'brilliant jerks' by ditching an out-of-date grading system. To create the most holistic view, they separated performance levels into three assessment areas which are weighed equally when creating performance ratings. These include expectations of the role, contribution to the team and demonstration of company values.[2]

Atlassian updated their performance process so that employees receive one of three grade levels on each element, based on growth mindset language. Rather than a score, they get an exceptional year, a great year, or an off year.[3]

This system ensures technical capabilities are measured and also behavioural capabilities, which link to values and mindset.

You hired your mates

It's likely that in the early days you hired your mates, your garage band. It's possible that they have now reached the peak of their capability, they don't have the potential to scale with your business, and they're no longer working out. But you don't want to let them go. They were with you at the start, and they're loyal. They're your mates!

In his biography of Steve Jobs, Walter Isaacson discusses how Jobs prevented what he called 'the bozo explosion' by not tolerating managers who allowed mediocre people to stick around. Jobs said, 'If something sucks, I tell people to their face. It's my job to be honest.'[4]

While I'm not condoning this blunt approach, I encourage you to consider the impact of poor performance and lack of capability on the rest of the team. You may be ignoring that while these 'mates' cannot do their jobs and others have to pick up the slack, they are also probably becoming disgruntled. They're no longer in the inner circle and feel they are losing ownership. They are making life miserable for everyone around them.

So, would you hire that person today?

Be a legend and let them go! It's time to make a tough call. And that means *you* make that call.

THE
SMARTEST
PEOPLE
ARE NOT
ALWAYS
THE
RIGHT
PEOPLE

The smartest people are not always the right people

As we identified earlier in the roadblocks, when hiring people for your high-growth business, there is a common temptation to appoint the smartest people. But hiring the best and the brightest people, who are typically at the highest salary levels, is a bad idea for many reasons:

> They absorb a lot of the limited available salary pool that could be allocated far more effectively. They take on non-essential, non-important work – just because they can do it and they enjoy it. Eventually, they get frustrated doing lower-level work. They get bored and restless and can become disruptive. They are typically not good at collaborating, preferring to work in their own way. Ultimately, they can become difficult to manage.

Instead of looking for the (traditionally) smartest people, consider what capabilities your business really needs. How does your hiring process align with your business strategy? Consider both technical and behavioural capabilities.

In addition to not just hiring the smartest person, consider what else applies to the role. Hire for the level of the role you need. If it's not a people leader role, don't share it as a leadership position. If it's a role that works independently, don't request someone who is high energy and collaborative.

There are some situations when hiring outside the specifics of a role can be the right option. For example, if a person is hired specifically to address a short-term future need (such as expertise in a particular ERP platform). Another example is if a person has clear potential and, with some development, could step up into a more senior position to meet a future need.

The whole curve

The current talent shortage is making hiring the right person more difficult. To broaden your options, bring an intentional focus to your search for diversity of gender, ethnicity, age, and neurodiversity, as well as diversity of thinking and behaviour. Leaders who don't lead from the heart are always going to struggle.

Engaging with a broader pool of talent, the whole bell curve, not just the obvious, easy-to-hire talent, can bring unexpected rewards.

In *What the Hell Do We Do Now?*, Callum McKirdy writes about embracing neurodiversity. 'It is from the edges of the bell curve that innovation has occurred. We simply assumed the leaders of innovation have been rare geniuses – and they have been. Yet, many more of these genius minds lay hidden among our workforces because where you have a difference, you have an ability to make a difference.'[5]

Resist the temptation to react to referrals of people you know are not who or what you need.

The Goterra Story

I recently spoke with Olympia Yarger, founder and CEO of Goterra, a waste management infrastructure business based in Canberra, Australia. Olympia has a global vision to decentralise food waste management with insect-powered, smart city infrastructure. Goterra has a fascinating history of attracting and engaging a diverse workforce.

Early in growing Goterra, staff were primarily interns and highly skilled immigrants whose qualifications weren't recognised in Australia. Both the business and the people had a need that matched. Unfortunately, this wasn't scalable as they were limited by work visas. Yarger commented that 'the burden on founders is to find people who want to come and do shit tons of work for not a lot of money'.

By connecting and engaging with the right organisations, like the Red Cross, Goterra also actively hires refugees. Olympia says that 'hiring immigrants and refugees needs extra consideration, because it involves a lot of paperwork, a lot of meetings and a lot of interviews with the Red Cross. This cannot be tokenism.'

I recalled a story from Goterra's first year that Olympia shared on Twitter. The company had advertised for an engineer and received 200 applicants. All male. Acknowledging that waste management is not at the pretty end of the work scale, Olympia challenged the assumption that only men would be interested in the role. Today (June 2022), Goterra's staff comprises thirty-seven per cent women, sixty per cent bilingual and from broad ethnic representation, and twenty-seven per cent people working with a disability.

Recognising that women are thirty per cent less likely to be progressed in a hiring process than men, another initiative the company engages in is to allow women applicants for graduate positions to progress to the final interview stage. This creates the opportunity for women to experience the hiring process, which may not result in a successful application but provides valuable experience to candidates. Goterra champions women and minorities in their marketing and actions to truly engage and demonstrate their intentions. A recent advertisement for a senior engineer had twenty-five per cent women applicants.

Olympia says, 'What's difficult is managing a good culture in among difficult work. A purposeful culture that scales takes effort.' I asked what she believed were the benefits of a diverse workforce. 'It brings degrees of perspective. A team that has created a place where people can work with a disability or that embraces minorities is a team that communicates better. It forces us not to make assumptions or take liberties with our privilege. It's the affirmation of the picture you had in your head of the work you wanted to create or the place you wanted to create for people to do amazing work, and it's succeeding. Those are the best days.'

Avoid costly hiring mistakes

*'Hiring is a network effect. The first 100
people you hire will define the next 200.'*

– Molly Graham (ex-early Google and Facebook)[6]

Hiring mistakes can cost your business in many ways. Firstly, there is the financial cost of hiring. For those doing the hiring, it's a waste of time, energy, and effort. It is bad for team morale and can be disruptive and unsettling.

Then, there is lost productivity and time needed to re-train the next hire. Hiring mistakes can damage the reputation of your business and make hiring even more challenging in the current global talent shortage.

Reporting on a 2021 online study, Robert Half Talent Solutions found that the impact of a bad hire among technology professionals is felt more acutely than in other sectors. A bad director-level tech hire costs nearly a quarter more than their initial salary. That means a poor decision to hire someone at AU$150k could cost you more than AU$35k.[7]

You can avoid making these costly mistakes.

Six reasons why you'll make hiring mistakes

1. Your hiring plan (if there is one) is not aligned with any business objective.
2. You hire to achieve a short-term focus.
3. You need people quickly, so you hire fast and fire slow. Or you have not fired and are still carrying the wrong people.
4. There are no criteria for hiring, and you're not taking an holistic approach. For example, hiring for technical skills but not accounting for behavioural skills or experience, because that part of the process is deemed too expensive.
5. Giving in to the temptation to rehire the mistakes, replacing old with new versions of the wrong people.
6. When you need an expert, you hire for lack of weakness rather than for strengths.[8] This is even more common when hiring is by consensus.

And the six fixes

1. Develop hiring plans as part of your people strategy. These plans need to align with your business strategy.
2. Take a more holistic approach to hiring. Become more discerning about who you're hiring. Know the type of person you'd like to work with. Understand what they value and how they engage with others. Don't just hire for technical skills.
3. Hire slow (cautiously), and fire fast.
4. When someone leaves, review what's really needed in the team. Do you need someone with those same skills, working the same way? Unlikely. Maybe you need someone who can step up into a people leadership role. And perhaps someone else in the team can absorb some of the work. Look at your

options before you jump in to replace like with like, aka the 'cloning effect'.

5. Before you hire, consider who you are carrying — those who no longer serve your business. Maybe it's time to make some tough calls and have a team reshuffle.

6. Be positively aware of the strengths of new hires. You have your list of role requirements, but what else can someone bring to your business? What diversity of action, behaviour, and thinking can they bring? Who do they know in the community? What relevant experience do they have from other companies? What expertise can they bring that will be useful in future? Be careful not to get swept up in any hype of expertise that's not relevant.

With high growth and so many urgent demands and distractions, it's challenging to step back and truly understand the capabilities you want to bring to your team. But given a potential cost of up to twenty-five per cent of an employee's salary, can you really afford to continue to make these hiring mistakes?

Steve Gard, founder of The Circle Back Initiative and BenchmarCX, shared in a LinkedIn post (April 2022) that a survey of more than 160 candidates revealed the following reasons for dropping out of the recruitment process. Thirty-eight per cent went with a company that moved quicker, and thirty-four per cent didn't stick it out because of poor candidate experience, while only nineteen per cent dropped out due to salary mismatch.[9]

You cannot be a casualty of this situation. Get moving and put a robust recruitment process in place.

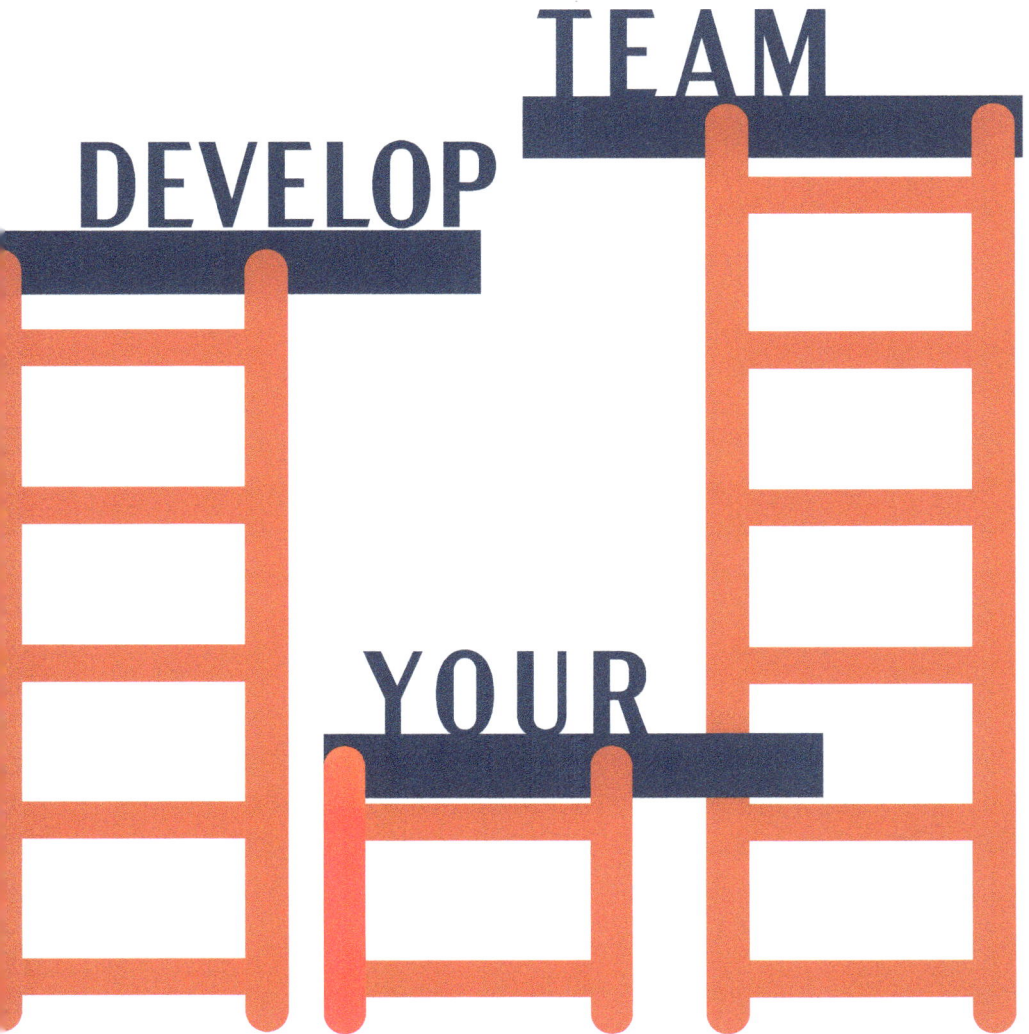

DEVELOP YOUR TEAM

Develop your team

A legendary leader has the ability to develop the team, delegate, educate, inform, empower, encourage, create an emotional connection, and be inclusive.

Developing your team is important for so many reasons. The effort delivers the results – tenfold. When people are given the opportunity to develop in their current role or into a future role, there is greater employee satisfaction. People feel valued when developing and leveraging their strengths, as it improves self-awareness and reduces blind spots.

The business benefits from people being more engaged and more likely to stay with your business. There is a reduced cost of hiring and retraining. Performance and productivity are improved, as people are more capable of doing their work and delivering their goals. You are building bench strength for the future. It enables a culture of trust and loyalty.

Do your best

Legendary leaders are not scared of development conversations. No one expects you to have all the answers — they just need you to care and make an effort. People are far more concerned with their careers than with you giving them wrong advice. Sometimes they just want to bounce ideas around or have you as a sounding board. You're not a career coach, but you can provide support.

'What if I promise them something we can't deliver? What if I don't know how to help them? What if....' Here are some common concerns that leaders have about developing their team or career conversations:

What if you promise them something you can't deliver?

> " You say: We'll do our best to make this happen for you but know that things are a little uncertain in this environment. Let's do what we can. Here's what I'll do. I'll talk to (relevant person), and let's see if there's a project we can get you involved in. Let me know how things progress. How committed are you, and what will you do to make it happen? "

What if they want to be a future leader but are not good with people or don't want to lead?

> " You say: There is always an opportunity for you to grow and succeed within this business. That future does not have to mean leading a team of people. This business provides opportunities for people with technical capabilities to pursue careers where people leadership is not a requirement. Let me know what kind of work you'd like to do and what you're good at. "

What if they want to study something that's not relevant to their role?

> " You say: This sounds great; it's interesting that you like this field of thinking. While I'd love to help you, can you tell me where you feel this is relevant to your role? If it is, we can make some time for you to study. If not, I'm afraid we cannot support you in this in terms of time or financial support, but I'd love to hear how you go if you pursue it outside your regular work. Let me know if I can help. "

What if you don't know how to help them?

> You say: I'm not the expert on this topic, but it sounds great. I'd love to help. Do you know someone who can help? Can I introduce you to someone who can help? Maybe we can make some time in your week to make this happen? Let me know what I can do.

A ready successor

People leaders have often shared with me that they don't want a successor or to develop a team member to step into their role. They're afraid that one day that person will take over, and they'll become redundant.

Having a ready successor is the best thing for your career. Even if they're not ready now, know who you'd like to step into your role one day and work to get them ready. Go back to Phase Three in Part Five for more information on planning for this.

There are real advantages to having a successor. They enable you to take a break, they free you up to get involved in innovative new projects, and they mean you can take a promotion when it arises. Being lined up as a successor is a great retention opportunity for your high performers. And finally, having a successor mitigates any risk to the business of having a gap if you leave or move on.

Best kept secret

EVP stands for Employee Value Proposition. If you want the right people in your business, with the skills and capability you require, whose values align with yours, and are passionate about your company, you'll need a really strong EVP.

And you'll need to make it visible internally to your employees and externally to the market.

Why an EVP matters

Almost every scaleup I've spoken with is not happy with their EVP. Why? They don't understand its importance, so they don't make any effort to get it right.

In May 2021, Gartner reported that only thirty-one per cent of HR leaders think their employees are satisfied with the EVP... (and) sixty-five per cent of candidates report that they have actually discontinued a hiring process due to an unattractive EVP.'[10]

Oh, I hear you say, but we have the best and coolest tech. Of course people will want to work here. Uh, no, that's not enough.

In the Korn Ferry Briefing, *What's in it for me?*[11] Russell Pearlman shares the demands of candidates due to shifts in work arrangements in recent years and the scarcity of talent. People now have new demands, and you ignore this at your peril.

According to Pearlman (US) candidates want more than just higher wages. They want more defined career paths, more training, hybrid work schedules, and full-time remote flexibility with more paid time off. They also want to do meaningful work for companies with a vocal stance on social issues.

You will need to demonstrate to potential candidates that you can provide these, or you'll risk having many gaps in talent.

Share your vision

People want to be able to connect to your vision, and they can only do that if they can *see* it.

Your vision is not just for internal employees. It is an essential tool in attracting new talent. Make it very clear on your website. People will connect to it, particularly if it connects to their purpose too.

Here are some great examples:

Disney: To make people happy.

Instagram: Give people the power to build community and bring the world closer together.

Tesla: To accelerate the world's transition to sustainable energy.

RSPCA Australia: To prevent cruelty to animals by actively promoting their care and protection.

Why are you keeping your vision a secret? It just doesn't make sense!

Canva's website declares: 'Sometimes the chance comes up to be part of something really special. Canva is making design amazingly simple for everyone, and the potential is limitless. We're empowering people to design anything and publish anywhere.'

Another example is the Australian shipping service company, Sendle. Their values are clear and simple. They are not generic, and they represent the brand. Sendle knows their people stats, and they keep them up to date. I know because I asked. For example, twenty-four per cent of their people are LGBTQIA+. They speak over twenty languages, and fifty per cent of their leaders and managers are women.

They are conscious of the environment. 'Sendle is Australia's first 100% carbon neutral shipping service.' They care about people, and it's not just lip service. 'People are what make Sendle work.' They share stories about their customers and the 'awesome people behind Sendle' – their employees.

Only men in STEM

A global tech company I worked with a few years ago was growing rapidly. They had engaged a single recruitment agency that, over the years, had developed a monopoly over their recruitment requirements. The client had no internal capacity to support a progressive recruitment process or to update the engagement with the agency. As their company requirements grew, there was no economy of scale, so it became an expensive arrangement.

In addition, there was only a technical test to complete. There were no behavioural or culture questions in the interview. As a result, there was very little diversity in the team. When I spoke with the client, they had hired all male engineers.

When I questioned this, I was told, 'there aren't any women in STEM'. *gasp

The lesson here is that the company had assumed that only males apply for STEM roles. They had cool tech that they believed should be enough to attract talent, and if women weren't applying it must be because they weren't suitable. They felt there was no point in focusing on gender, race, age, neurodiversity etc. They also believed that there was an over-supply of talent, so there was no need to try to actively attract candidates.

When an external party completed a health check on their recruitment process, it was discovered that AU$200k was spent with this agency in the previous twelve months. This revelation prompted a mindset shift to think differently about their approach. The company now has a part-time, in-house recruiter who works with various select agencies to ensure the right candidates are attracted to the business, and old assumptions about attraction and recruitment are no longer roadblocks.

Engagement is a business responsibility

> " 'Employees who are not engaged or who are actively disengaged cost the world US$7.8 trillion in lost productivity, according to Gallup's State of the Global Workplace: 2022 Report. That's equal to 11% of global GDP.'[12] "

Earlier I mentioned interviewing twenty Australian startups to learn how they had tried to overcome these roadblocks and improve hiring and engagement. Here's what they shared that had worked. For hiring, some felt that having transparent interviewing (the warts and all approach), effective recruiting processes, and appropriate onboarding were working for them. Collaborative office space, flexibility in work arrangements, and ESOP (Employee Share Ownership Plans) programs helped with attraction and hiring. For engagement, having a defined culture, mission and values, greater role autonomy with creative control, clear back-to-office plans, and a supportive rewards strategy were key.

Everyone is responsible for employee engagement. It's a business priority. The following tools are free, requiring only care and attention to do the right thing by your team. And that is what people want and need to remain loyal to you and your growing business. With the growing competition for talent, it's important to focus on these opportunities for improved engagement and retention.

There are six levers for engagement

For your team to feel engaged, they should experience each of these levers.

Engaged — feel listened to

Find opportunities to seek their input. Respond to their suggestions.

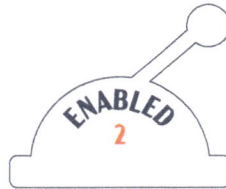

Enabled — have the tools and the resources to do the job

Make technology and equipment available. Minimise distractions such as meetings and, where possible, reduce the workload.

Empowered — have no unnecessary restrictions

Let them make decisions, don't be a bottleneck. Give them autonomy to do their job.

Encouraged — feel supported and motivated

Provide opportunities for growth and development. Create an environment for reward and recognition, and share the good news stories.

Educated — feel informed and understand expectations

People need to know what's expected of them. Communicate regularly and clearly, sharing the strategy expectations.

Emotionally connected — see the impact of their efforts

Align people's strengths and interests with their work. People need to feel connected to a sense of purpose and be excited and energised by their work.

According to the Employee Engagement Statistics 2022 (US) report, 'While 60% of employers have increased employee listening efforts, few are using formal listening approaches. Indeed, just 31% conduct employee surveys and 13% conduct focus groups.'[13]

Legend List

1   Work through the four phases of building the right team structure.

2   Who are the 'wrong' people you are holding on to? How will you make the tough calls to implement team changes?

3   Develop a strong EVP and engagement strategy to retain the right people in your business.

NOW YOU CHOOSE:

LIABILITY

OR

LEGEND?

Over to you

Do you want to invest in yourself to become a legendary leader? Someone who regularly engages with your team, building trust and connection. Someone who seeks feedback to continually improve, lift capability and become a better leader.

A legendary leader is known for leading strategically. They know who they are, what they want and how they will do it. They develop a culture that aligns with their vision and values.

They have clear role boundaries and extend that role clarity to the whole team.

They have solid, trusting relationships. They are not afraid to ask for help.

They take time to build the right team to deliver on the business strategy.

Invest in you

It's your choice.

There are plenty of consultants who will help you take the easy approach and dilute the outcome. But if you want to make the tough but necessary calls to become a legendary leader and put your business on a trajectory to success, I'll support you all the way.

If you'd like to learn how to become a legendary leader instead of a liability to your business, I'd love to have a chat.

References

Introduction

1. CB Insights. 2022, June 14. The top 20 reasons startups fail. https://s3-us-west-2.amazonaws.com/cbi-content/research-reports/The-20-Reasons-Startups-Fail.pdf

2. Pride, Jamie. 2018. *Unicorn Tears. Why startups fail and how to avoid it*. Milton, QLD, Australia. Wiley.

3. Eisenmann, Tom. 2021. *The Fail-Safe Startup: Your Roadmap for Entrepreneurial Success*. London: Penguin.

4. Aulet, Bill. 2013. *Disciplined Entrepreneurship. Hoboken, N.J.: Wiley*.

5. Love, Howard. 2016. *The Start-up J curve: The six steps to entrepreneurial success*. Austin, Texas: Greenleaf Book Group Press.

6. Rose, David S. 2016. *The Startup Checklist: 25 steps to a scalable, high-growth business*. Hoboken, N.J.: Wiley.

7. Ries, Eric. 2011. *The Lean Startup: How relentless change creates radically successful businesses*. Penguin Random House UK.

8. Byrne, John A. 2013. Sheryl Sandberg's Inspiring Speech at Harvard Business School. https://www.linkedin.com/pulse/20130417200657-17970806-sheryl-sandberg-s-inspiring-speech-at-harvard-business-school/

9. Burnison, Gary. 2022, January 12. Our Time of Change, Insights. *Korn Ferry*. https://www.kornferry.com/insights/special-edition/our-time-of-change

10. Kotashev, Kyril. 2022, January 9. Startup failure rate. *Failory*. https://www.failory.com/blog/startup-failure-rate

11. Davidson, John. 2021, June 29. Skills crisis pushes up tech wages by a third. *Australian Financial Review*. https://www.afr.

com/technology/skills-crisis-pushes-up-tech-wages-by-a-third-20210627-p584po

12. Grohl, Dave. 2021. *The Storyteller: Tales of Life and Music*. London: Simon & Schuster.

13. Richardson, Saul. 2020, February 28. A sequence of levels of development in learning jazz improvisation. *Jazz Workshop*. https://jazzworkshopaustralia.com.au/a-sequence-of-levels-of-development-in-learning-jazz-improvisation/

14. Graham, Molly. n.d. 'Give Away Your Legos' and Other Commandments for Scaling Startups. *First Round Review*. https://review.firstround.com/give-away-your-legos-and-other-commandments-for-scaling-startups

15. McKeown, Greg. 2022, May 26. The Essentialist. *LinkedIn*. https://www.linkedin.com/pulse/have-you-ever-won-wrong-race-greg-mckeown/?trackingId=vaXZln3pmLWmC%2BUTNBLiQg%3D%3D

Part One

1. Pressfield, Steven. 2012. *Turning Pro: tap your inner power and create your life's work*. New York: Black Irish Entertainment.

2. Harnish, Verne. 2014. *Scaling up: how a few companies make it...and why the rest don't*. Ashburn, Virginia: Gazelles Inc.

3. Tekir, Arzu. 2020, February 11. Culture Matters: How Great Startups Will Thrive In 2020. *Forbes*. https://www.forbes.com/sites/ellevate/2020/02/11/culture-matters-how-great-startups-will-thrive-in-2020/#

4. Horowitz, Ben. 2014. *The Hard Thing About Hard Things*. New York: HarperCollins.

5. Australian Bureau of Statistics. Media Release. 2022, June 8. Close to 3% of jobs vacant in March quarter. *Labour Account Australia*. https://www.abs.gov.au/media-centre/media-releases/close-3-jobs-vacant-march-quarter

Part Two

1. Godin, Seth. 2010. *Linchpin: Are you indispensible?* New York: Portfolio.

2. Grant, Adam. 2022. *Think Again: The power of knowing what you don't know.* London: Random House.

3. Pressfield, Steven. 2012. *Turning Pro: tap your inner power and create your life's work.* New York: Black Irish Entertainment.

Part Three

1. Clear, James. 2020, May 14. 3-2-1: Entrepreneurship, habits, and the joy of climbing. https://jamesclear.com/3-2-1/may-14-2020

2. Wasserman, Noam. 2013. *The Founder's Dilemmas: anticipating and avoiding the pitfalls that can sink a startup.* Princeton, N.J.: Princeton University Press.

3. Palmer-Derrien, Stephanie. 2018, May 28. "No bullshit": Atlassian's Dom Price shares four key ingredients for scaling a startup. *Smart Company.* https://www.smartcompany.com.au/startupsmart/advice/atlassian-dom-price-four-key-ingredients-for-scaling-startup-successfully/

4. Pink, Daniel H. 2009. *Drive: the surprising truth about what motivates us.* New York: Riverhead Books.

5. Ficarra, Glenn and Requa, John. 2022. WeCrashed. *Apple TV+.*

6. Pietsch, Brian. 2020, May. WeWork's valuation fell from $47 billion last year to $2.9 billion. *Business Insider.* https://www.businessinsider.com/wework-valuation-falls-47-billion-to-less-than-3-billion-2020-5

7. Blystone, Dan. 2021, September 19. The Story of Uber. *Investopedia.* https://www.investopedia.com/articles/personal-finance/111015/story-uber.asp

8. Coulter, Alan. 2022. Super Pumped. *Paramount Global Distribution Group.* Showtime.

9. Dell, Michael. 2021. *Play Nice But Win.* New York: Penguin Random House.

10. Desmond-Harris, Jenee. 2021. https://twitter.com/jdesmondharris/status/1408868731707555840

11. McKeown, Greg. 2014. *Essentialism: The disciplined pursuit of less.* New York: Crown Business.

12. Clear, James. 2018. *Atomic Habits: tiny changes, remarkable results: an easy & proven way to build good habits & break bad ones.* New York: Avery.

Part Four

1. Horowitz, Ben. 2019. *What You Do is Who You Are: How to create your business culture.* New York: HarperBusiness.

2. Newton Ph.D., Rebecca. 2016, November 2. HR Can't Change Company Culture by Itself. *Harvard Business Review.* https://hbr.org/2016/11/hr-cant-change-company-culture-by-itself

3. Fried, Jason and Heinemeier Hansson, David. 2010. *Rework.* New York: Penguin Random House LLC.

4. Sundaram, Dipak and Patel, Niraj. 2019, January 31. Essential Ingredients for an Effective Onboarding Program for Gallup. *Gallup.* https://www.gallup.com/workplace/246242/essential-ingredients-effective-onboarding-program.aspx

5. Whispir. 2022, June 1. The cost of not communicating: How Whispir's tailored messaging tech lifts engagement. *Business News Week.* https://www.businessnewsaustralia.com/blog/the-cost-of-not-communicating--how-whispir-s-tailored-messaging-tech-lifts-engagement

Part Five

1. Palmer-Derrien, Stephanie. 2018, May 28. "No bullshit": Atlassian's Dom Price shares four key ingredients for scaling a startup. *Smart Company.* https://www.smartcompany.com.au/startupsmart/advice/atlassian-dom-price-four-key-ingredients-for-scaling-startup-successfully/

2. Chee, Bek. 2019, July 18. What you should really measure in your annual performance reviews (and why). *Work Life.* https://www.atlassian.com/blog/hr-teams/our-performance-reviews-framework

3. Chung, Frank. 2019, July 19. Atlassian ditches 'brilliant jerks' in performance review overhaul. *news.com.au*. https://www.news.com.au/finance/work/at-work/atlassian-ditches-brilliant-jerks-in-performance-review-overhaul/news-story/82a5e2abba1939f51d68a e81db8f05bd

4. Isaacson, Walter. 2015. *Steve Jobs*. New York: Simon & Schuster.

5. McKirdy, Callum. 2020. *What the hell do we do now? An enterprise guide to Covid-19 and beyond.* In Butler, M., Hagan, A., Hodgson, B., et. al. Victoria: Kienco Pty.

6. Graham, Molly. n.d. 'Give Away Your Legos' and Other Commandments for Scaling Startups. *First Round Review*. https://review.firstround.com/give-away-your-legos-and-other-commandments-for-scaling-startups

7. Robert Half Talent Solutions. 2021, August, 2. *The rising costs of a bad hire*. https://www.roberthalf.com.au/press/rising-costs-bad-hire

8. Horowitz, Ben. 2014. *The Hard Thing About Hard Things*. New York: HarperCollins.

9. Gard, Steve. 2022, April. The Circle Back Initiative. *LinkedIn*. https://www.linkedin.com/posts/steve-gard_jobs-careers-recruitment-activity-6924116143792173057-rR4s?utm_source=linkedin_share&utm_medium=member_desktop_web

10. Venkataramani, Swetha. 2021, May 13. Make Way For a More Human-Centric Employee Value Proposition. *Gartner Insights*. https://www.gartner.com/smarterwithgartner/make-way-for-a-more-human-centric-employee-value-proposition.

11. Pearlman, Russell. 2021, July 29. What's in it for me? *Korn Ferry Briefings Magazine*. https://www.kornferry.com/insights/briefings-magazine/issue-50/whats-in-it-for-me

12. Pendall, Ryan. 2022, June 14. The World's $7.8 Trillion Workplace Problem. *Gallup*. https://www.gallup.com/workplace/393497/world-trillion-workplace-problem.aspx

13. Bennet, Steve. 2022, May 13. Employee Engagement Statistics 2022 -Everything You Need to Know. https://webinarcare.com/best-employee-engagement-software/employee-engagement-statistics/

www.ingramcontent.com/pod-product-compliance
Lightning Source LLC
Chambersburg PA
CBHW040921210326
41597CB00030B/5150

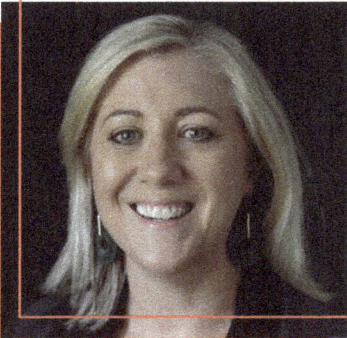

Mary Butler

Legendary Leadership Coach

**I get what traditional HR doesn't.
And I get scaleups.**

You're an expert in your space, so let me be your expert in people strategy. I see what people do best and help them do it better.

I have more than twenty-five years of talent management experience, from global corporates to scaleups in every sector. I've worked across Europe, the USA, Asia, and Australia in aviation, tech, and professional services industries. That's deep expertise across a broad range of leadership topics we can leverage in your business.

While I have a BSc and an MBA, my ability to identify and address those often-buried challenges makes me different. I don't offer an off-the-shelf solution to a problem we haven't even discussed.

One of my clients described me as someone whose 'charming style belies an ability to ask the difficult questions of an organisation, its founders, managers, and directors. Before you know it, you are opening up and dealing with the hard issues.'

Scan here to discover my Legendary Leadership diagnostic and learn more about my work.

www.marybutler.net

linkedin.com/in/marybutlerpeoplestrategy